John Paterson Smyth

Our Bible in the Making

As seen by modern research

John Paterson Smyth

Our Bible in the Making
As seen by modern research

ISBN/EAN: 9783337172251

Printed in Europe, USA, Canada, Australia, Japan

Cover: Foto ©Lupo / pixelio.de

More available books at **www.hansebooks.com**

OUR BIBLE IN THE MAKING

AS SEEN BY MODERN RESEARCH

BY

J. PATERSON SMYTH
B.D., LITT.D., D.C.L.

ARCHDEACON OF ST. ANDREW'S, MONTREAL; LATE PROFESSOR OF
PASTORAL THEOLOGY, UNIVERSITY OF DUBLIN

AUTHOR OF "HOW WE GOT OUR BIBLE," "THE OLD DOCUMENTS
AND THE NEW BIBLE," "THE GOSPEL OF THE
HEREAFTER" ETC.

LONDON

CONTENTS

PROLOGUE

		PAGE
I.	The Church and the Bible	3
II.	The Appeal of the Bible	14
III.	Criticism and the Bible	29

THE MAKING OF THE OLD TESTAMENT

I.	The Lost Library	41
II.	Some Contents of the Lost Library	49
III.	The "Bibles before the Bible"	76
IV.	The Recovery of the Lost Bibles	91
V.	The Canon of the Old Testament	99
VI.	The Completed Jewish Bible	117

THE APOCRYPHA

The Apocryphal Books	135
The Apocrypha in the Jewish Bible	141
The Apocrypha in the Christian Church	147

THE MAKING OF THE NEW TESTAMENT

I.	The New Testament in the Making	159
II.	The Canon of the New Testament	185

LIST OF ILLUSTRATIONS

	TO FACE PAGE
PHOTOGRAPH OF ANCIENT GREEK MANUSCRIPTS *Frontispiece*	
FRAGMENTS OF THE DELUGE TABLETS, THE ELEVENTH TABLET OF THE EPIC OF GILGAMESH CONTAINING THE DELUGE STORY	52
THE BLACK DIORITE BLOCK FOUND IN SUSA, 1901, REPRESENTING KING HAMMURABI RECEIVING THE LAWS FROM HIS GOD	72
ARCHBISHOP AELFRIC'S ANGLO-SAXON BIBLE, ELEVENTH CENTURY.	130
NEW "SAYINGS OF JESUS." *Papyrus from Oxyrhynchus, now in the British Museum*	174
THE SINAITIC MANUSCRIPT	208

PART I
PROLOGUE

PROLOGUE

CHAPTER I

THE CHURCH AND THE BIBLE

I

How the Church formed the Bible.

RECENTLY a thoughtful, devout layman said to the writer, "I never read the Old Testament now, as I feel that the results of modern scholarship have entirely upset for me its foundations as an inspired book."

This is a very dangerous misunderstanding and unfortunately a widespread one. It is futile to hide our heads in the sand and imagine that people are not disturbed about it. And it is equally futile to decry the critical studies which have caused the disturbance. For our best Christian scholars are now agreed that the main central results of critical scholarship have come to stay.

The aim of this book is to arouse interest and remove misunderstanding by telling the story of the making of the Bible simply and frankly in the light of modern scholarship. For it is a very interesting and helpful story. There is nothing really disquieting in it. Nay, rather, when we have got over the disturbance caused by shifting our point of view, it should make the Bible for us a more living, throbbing human presentation of God. People talk of the Bible coming down from its pedestal as a result of modern research. Perhaps in a sense it is true. Old classic legends tell of the young sculptor who carved his statue of surpassing beauty and then, as he gazed at it on its pedestal, fell in love with the work of his own hands. He prayed to the gods to give life to his creation, and lo! as he prayed came stirring breath and colour, and at length it came down into his arms, a living, throbbing woman to be his joy and companion and comfort in his daily life. If the fuller light which has fallen on the story of the Bible should tend in any degree to bring it down from the conventional pedestal on which verbal inspiration and such like theories have placed it, may it not be to bring it closer to our hearts and make us feel more truly behind it the real, living, throbbing spirit of God, who inspired it?

The story of the making of the Bible is a very different thing from the story of how we got our Bible, which in our day has been told by many writers in popular form. This latter begins with the early manuscripts of our present Scriptures and traces their history down through the centuries till they appear in the printed collection of books which we now call the Bible. But the mind naturally gropes further back—and the recent disquiet about Higher Criticism adds force to its questionings :—

How did we originally get this collection of books—history and biography and letters and sermons and poetry and drama? When and where was the ultimate beginning of them? Had they any existence before they were written in the Bible? Who wrote them? Who collected them? Who selected them? By what test were they selected out of the literature of the time? For there was a wider literature. Other books beside these were written by "holy men of old," both in Old Testament and New Testament times. How does it happen that these particular books and no other should be regarded as specially inspired and collected into an authoritative Bible?

§ 2. It will simplify the answer if it be kept clearly in mind that there are two stages in the making of the Bible.

First. The gradual growth of a religious literature.

Second. The selection or acceptance or recognition of certain parts of that literature as authoritative and inspired Scripture.

These stages must be kept clearly distinct, and always there must be kept prominently in mind the thought of a religious community behind them. The growth of a religious literature suggests the thought of a religious community in which it grew. The selection of any literature to make into a Bible implies that there must have been behind that literature a religious community to select it. That goes without saying. It is impossible to discuss the subject at all until we recognize the fact that the Bible does not stand alone. A divine society, divinely formed and guided and inspired, stands behind it. In this divine society it grew from small beginnings away far back in dim antiquity. By this divine society it was selected and guarded and transmitted. The Bible is the Book of the Church, and the question of its growth and formation is quite an impossible one if it be thought of apart from the background of the Church.

The Church stands behind the Bible. The Jewish Church stands behind the Old Testament. The Christian Church stands behind the New

Testament. The law and the prophets and the psalms did not drop down from heaven promiscuously into the world. God selected a certain community, a certain religious society in which these books grew and were written and selected and preserved and transmitted for the world's good. Our Lord did not first give us the Gospels and Epistles and then appoint apostles and disciples to lecture about them. He first founded a divine society, the Church, and at His Ascension He left to the world not the Gospels and Epistles but this divine society with its fellowship and its mysterious, spirit-guided life, and afterwards as the occasion arose the members of this divine society were inspired to write the Gospels and Epistles.

"There is no true antithesis between the Church and the Bible. The Bible is really the voice of the Church in its first and greatest age. However much and however rightly we may elevate the authority of Prophets and Wise Men and Apostles, that authority does not belong to them either as speaking or writing in isolation. They are always in closest touch with the Church of their day, and they draw spiritual sustenance from the contact —even though they give it back in redoubled measure. . . . Inspiration should be thought of as acting through (the Church) here weakly, there strongly, but yet in different degrees permeating the whole.[1]

§ 3. This then is the first step in the making of the Bible. God in His loving purpose for the world's blessing and good selected through His divine providence a community of men in which His Holy Spirit should especially act, not for their sakes alone but for the sake of the whole world. In this community both in Old and New Testament times was an all-pervading sense of God's presence and rule. In it arose prophets and psalmists and apostles and teachers who in various degrees felt strongly the religious impulse to help life upward. They were not all of the same level—some were ordinary, commonplace good men—some had a very high inspiration, a very deep intuition of the grandeur of righteousness, of the hand of God behind all history. Thus there arose a religious literature and history. In this literature and history certain parts stood out more prominently, partly through great authors' names, mainly through the gradual popular recognition of higher spiritual values. Thus came a gradual, half-unconscious selection of what seemed highest and best—what most appealed to

---

[1] Sanday, *Inspiration*. Preface to third edition.

the highest and best in men, what they felt convinced in the deep recesses of their soul to be the expression of the mind of God. And this selection is the Bible.

Not all the utterances of patriarch, or prophet, or psalmist found a place in the Old Testament. Not all the lives of Jesus or writings of apostolic days appear in the New Testament. By the silent, mysterious guiding of the Holy Spirit the Church of God in Old Testament and New Testament days slowly and gradually formed the collection of books which we now call the Bible.

§ 4. In a very real sense then, the statement is true that the Church formed the Bible. But we must not misunderstand the statement. It does not mean that the Jewish or Christian Church on some definite occasion, on its own authority, officially selected from its literature certain books and decided that they were to be regarded as inspired and authoritative. On the other hand, neither does it mean that they had only to collect and safeguard certain books which from their ultimate beginnings stood apart from all their other literature, or whose divine origin was somehow miraculously guaranteed. There is an old Church fable that at the time of the Council of Nice all the books were placed near the altar with a prayer that God would decide between them, and that immediately the true canonical books of Scripture jumped up on the altar and the others remained quietly on the floor!

Some such process might fit in with popular notions about Scripture. But the divine method was very different, and here I call careful attention to this method. Not suddenly, by some startling miracle—not officially, by some decision of a council, but slowly, gradually, half unconsciously, by the quiet influence of the Holy Spirit on the minds of men in the Church, was the canon of Scripture settled. " The Bible was formed even as the Church itself was formed by that Holy Spirit which was the life of both." The Bible and the Church were correlative to each other. Neither was the Church without the Bible nor the Bible without the Church. The Holy Spirit, who touched the highest consciences in the community to utter noble teaching, touched also the general conscience of that community to discriminate between higher and lower—to appreciate and love and treasure especially what was highest and most valuable to its religious life. The formation of this collection of documents was gradual. It was decided unconsciously by usage rather than by criticism or deliberate choice. It was no verdict of any one gathering of men that formed the Bible. It was the slow, accumulating verdict of the ages.

§ 5. Does it seem derogatory to Holy Scripture to say that it was the judgment of men that made certain books into a Bible ? At any rate it was so. There is a mysterious upward look in poor fallen humanity made in God's image, touched by God's spirit. " We needs must love the highest when we see it," even though we may refuse to follow it. It was this response to the highest, specially quickened in a community under God's peculiar guidance, which made the Church recognize and appreciate and reverence and preserve certain books which seemed instinct with the Spirit of God.

The making of the Bible was the act of men. But surely it was none the less for that the act of God the Holy Spirit. It was really His divine working that separated certain books for the perpetual instruction of the Church. But the mode of His working was by the quickening and guiding of human souls, that they should instinctively love what was most divine, what was most stimulating and helpful to their religious life ; that by a divine impulse men should gradually arrive at a general recognition of a certain set of writings as authoritative and inspired Scripture. Thus the Bible formed itself by a power inherent in it. It won its own way. It built its own throne. All that was best in human consciousness recognized its right to rule over men. Its position, we repeat, rests on no external authority, on no sentence of council or synod or prophet or saint, but on a gradual choice by a Church guided by the Spirit of God.

§ 6. It is quite true, as we shall see later, that the representatives of the Jewish Church officially pronounced their verdict as to what books should be in the Old Testament canon of Scripture. Yes, but when? Somewhere about the time of our Lord, after the accepted books had been for centuries recognized as of God. It is quite true that the Christian Church collected certain New Testament writings to form their Bible. But when? After they had been for three hundred years accepted as the God-given guide of the Church.

Surely no one would say that the Books owe their position to the fact that the Church thus formally recognized and collected them into a Bible, any more than one would say that the works of

Shakespeare, or Browning, or Tennyson owe their position to the fact that we have placed them in our collections of standard English literature. The books of Scripture asserted their own position. It was not the Church's collecting them into a Bible that made them of authority but rather the fact of their possessing authority made them be collected into a Bible.

What gave them this authority?

CHAPTER II

THE APPEAL OF THE BIBLE

I

The Appeal of the Prophets.
WHAT gave them this authority? Why should any set of old documents have been for thousands of years accepted as of divine origin and yielded to by men as an authority to guide their conduct and impose on them commands often disagreeable to themselves? Remember that they were isolated utterances often with centuries intervening between them, coming from various authors of various characters to various sets of people under various circumstances—that they originated in small beginnings centuries behind our present Bible—that in many cases we do not know their origin, or their authors, or by what processes they assumed their present form—that they were marked off by no miracle, nor guaranteed by any formal decision of any external authority. And yet somehow we can never reach back in history to a time when they were not reverenced as in some degree at least above

human productions. There they stand, a long chain with one end reaching away into the far back past and the other end gathering around the feet of Christ.

What gave them their authority?

There seems no possible answer but that already suggested, that they possessed it of themselves. They commanded their position by a power inherent in them. Men's reason and spiritual sense combined to establish them. They appealed by their own intrinsic worth to the God-given moral faculty and the response to that appeal has been, through all the ages since, the real foundation of the Bible's position.

§ 2. Look at the Old Testament, where the question chiefly arises. If we are asked to-day why we receive it as inspired, the usual reply is that we receive it on the authority of Christ and His apostles. They accepted it as the word of God and handed it down with their imprimatur upon it. But that does not answer the question, for we want to know why it was accepted before their day without any such imprimatur.

Look first at the prophets. How did men come to believe and obey the words of Amos, and Isaiah, and Jeremiah, and the rest? No answer, we repeat, is possible but this, that they compelled recognition. There was no miracle to attest them, no council to authorize them, no audible voice from heaven to compel men's allegiance. The prophets asserted their deep conviction that God was behind their message, but they did not point to any outward confirmation, and men simply were forced to believe them. There was something in their messages which compelled the belief that they really were the word of the Lord. And the longer the Jewish nation lasted the more time there was for these utterances to produce their impression, the more thoroughly were they recognized by the conscience of the people as being of divine origin and authority.

§ 3. Now let us try to bring this conviction home to ourselves—*to test on ourselves* the power of these Scripture utterances which persuaded men of old that they came from above. For it is as they compel in us the same convictions that we can really understand the making of the Bible.

Get outside all thoughts of an authoritative Bible, get back into the days when it was only in the making. Forget the fuller light of Christ in which you stand, which reveals comparative imperfections in those ancient writers. Put yourself in their place. Picture the nations of the earth in their ignorance and depravity, with their blind gropings after God, reaching no higher than fetishes and idols, and the tales of classical mythology. Then listen wonderingly to those prophetic voices in Israel amid the surroundings of that dark old world in the days before Romulus and Remus were suckled by the wolf:

"Jehovah, Jehovah. A God full of compassion and gracious, slow to anger and plenteous in mercy and truth, keeping mercy for thousands, forgiving iniquity, and transgression, and sin, and that will by no means clear the guilty.

"Rend your hearts and not your garments, and turn unto the Lord your God, for He is gracious and merciful, slow to anger and of great kindness and repenteth Him of the evil.

"Thus saith the high and holy One that inhabiteth eternity, whose name is Holy: I dwell in the high and holy place with him that is of a contrite and humble spirit, to revive the spirit of the humble and to revive the heart of the contrite one.

"What doth the Lord require of thee but to do justly and to love mercy and to walk humbly with thy God?

"How shall I give thee up, Ephraim, how shall I deliver thee, Israel? Mine heart is turned within Me and my compassions are kindled together."

And mingled with these noble thoughts, like a golden thread woven through the web of prophecy, see that strangely persistent groping after some great Being, some great purpose of God in the future —from the Genesis prediction of " The Seed of the Woman " to the vision of the Coming One by the great prophet of the exile—" Surely He hath borne our griefs and carried our sorrows—the Lord hath laid on Him the iniquity of us all."

Try to realize the impressiveness of it. All down the Jewish history in the midst of a dark world came these mysterious voices telling of a holy God—teaching, threatening, pleading, encouraging, pointing to a gradually brightening ideal and to the hope of some Great One who yet was to come. And to deepen its impressiveness notice that these prophets asserted passionately their conviction : " These are not our words. These are not our thoughts, God has put them into us. The Word of the Lord came unto me. Hear ye therefore the word of the Lord." How could the people doubt it ? They were not good people. They were " stiff-necked and uncircumcised in heart and ears, who did always resist the Holy Ghost." They hated the high teaching. They killed the prophets and stoned those who were sent unto them. But conscience insisted that these prophets were right and, by and by, in deep remorse they built them sepulchres and treasured up what fragments they could find of their sacred words. How could they help it? Put yourself in their place. Do you not feel that you must have done the same if you had been there?

II

The Appeal of the Psalms. The same is evidently true of the psalms, the hymns of the Jewish Church. They, too, owe their position to the appeal which they made to the highest in men. They were the utterances of noble souls who with all their imperfections knew and loved God, and all kindred souls then and since have felt their power in inspiring the spiritual life. The author's name did not matter. In most cases it was not known. They were at first isolated compositions. Gradually they grew into little collections. Just as in the case of our own hymns to-day some " caught on " and became favourites and survived, because of their deeper appeal to some side of the religious nature. Thus half unconsciously came a gradual sifting out. Their use in the temple strengthened their position. And so by degrees came the five little hymn books (as indicated in the Revised Version), which were afterwards brought together in our present collection.

The position of the Psalter, we repeat, is not due to any author's name, to any council's sanction, but to its compelling appeal to the highest side of men in that old Jewish Community. That was how the Holy Spirit wrought in making the Bible. Judged by the higher standard of Jesus Christ we can see imperfections and faults due to the poor imperfect men who wrote that Psalter. Strange if it were otherwise in that dark age in which it grew. But when all allowance has been made for these, who can doubt that that Psalter, which has been so powerful in inspiring human life through the ages since, caught on to men's souls in those early days and convinced them that it came from God?

Again let us test its compelling power on ourselves. Keep back still in that dim old world with its self-seeking, and idolatries, and human sacrifices, and lustful abominations, with no real sense of sin, no longings after holiness, and listen to the Jewish shepherd reciting in the field, and the Jewish choir boy singing in the church:

> " Praise the Lord, O my soul, and all that is within me, praise His Holy Name, Who forgiveth all thine iniquities, Who healeth all thy diseases. Who redeemeth

thy life from destruction, Who crowneth thee with loving kindness and tender mercies. . . . Like as a father pitieth his own children, so is the Lord merciful to them that fear Him, for He knoweth our frame, He remembereth that we are but dust.

"Lord, who shall sojourn in Thy tabernacle, who shall dwell in Thy holy hill? He that walketh uprightly and worketh righteousness and speaketh the truth in his heart.

"The Lord is my shepherd. I shall not want. He maketh me to lie down in green pastures, He leadeth me beside the still waters. He restoreth my soul. He leadeth me in the paths of righteousness for His Name's sake. Yea, though I walk through the valley of the shadow of death, I will fear no evil, for Thou art with me.

"Have mercy on me, O God, according to Thy loving kindness, according to the multitude of Thy tender mercies, blot out my transgressions. Wash me thoroughly from mine iniquity and cleanse me from my sin. . . . The sacrifices of God are a broken spirit, a broken and contrite heart, O God, Thou wilt not despise."

Are not such songs in such an age one of the great miracles of history? How could men help loving and reverencing and preserving such songs? How could they help feeling that a divine Spirit was behind them?

III

The Appeal of the History. The rest of the Old Testament is the history of God dealing with the nation—a story gathered under the guidance of God's providence in many generations, from many sources, since the far-back childhood of the race. At first sight the appeal to us seems decidedly weaker here than in the prophets and psalms. These historians had not our modern advantages. Much of their material came from old traditions and from various written records and collections of national songs and stories. So far as we can judge God's providence worked on natural lines. Evidently it is a true history in the main, but we have no right to assume that they were miraculously guarded from any inaccuracies of figure or fact in all these ancient sources, therefore we cannot claim infallibility for every detail.

The appealing power of their history consists in the fact that it is a revelation of God, a history of God's dealings with men. Underneath it all lies the deep conviction, the foundation of Israel's religion.

> The Lord our God is a righteous God, and righteousness is what He desires in His people.

This conviction had grown into the very blood

of the nation. It belonged not to prophets and historians alone, but to the whole community, however little they yielded to it.

No one will ever know who these writers were. One writer wrote this part, another wrote that, others later on edited and revised and combined. So the story grew. It was no one author's story. It was a story by a community dedicated to God, telling what He helped them to see of His relation toward them.

The historians were evidently men with a prophetic instinct. History was part of the work of the prophetic order. As we shall see later on in the early foundations of the Old Testament, the books from Joshua to Kings were known as "The Former Prophets," as distinguished from Isaiah, Jeremiah, Ezekiel, and the book of the Twelve, which were known as "The Latter Prophets." All prophets were not on the same high level. Obadiah hid a hundred prophets in a cave. There were many obscure prophets whose words we never hear of, simple, humble, religious men, who declared God's will and helped in their quiet way to build up the religious life of Israel. Amongst these unnamed ones were the men who generation after generation recorded and interpreted the history of the nation and showed God always behind it.

But we make no appeal on the score of their being prophets. The appeal is made by the history itself. Was ever national history so extraordinarily written? It is the history of an evil and rebellious people, yet everything is looked at in relation to the God of Righteousness. Records of other ancient nations tell what this or that great king accomplished, how the people conquered or were conquered by their enemies. In these Jewish records everything is of God—a righteous, holy God. It is God who conquered, God who delivered, God who punished, God who fought. There is no boasting of the national glory, no flattering of the national vanity; their greatest sins and disgraces and punishments are recorded just as fully as their triumphs and their joys. In the records of other nations the chief stress is laid on power and prosperity and comfort and wealth. In these strange records goodness seems to be the only thing of importance. To do the right, to please the holy God is of infinitely more value than to be powerful or rich or successful in life. "He did that which was right in the sight of the Lord." "He did that which was evil in the sight of the Lord," are the epitaphs of their most famous kings.

Therefore the national history of Israel also holds its position by its appeal to the religious instinct. No author's name, no theory of its composition affects its position. Whatever its imperfection it has impressed itself upon us as the simple story of God's dealing with men.

IV

The Appeal to Christ. Be it remembered that I am not here discussing with Christian men *our* reasons for believing in the inspiration of the Old Testament. I am but concerned with the story of the making of the Bible. I am trying to put myself back into the position of the old Jewish Church, trying to understand the compelling impulse which made them mark off certain books as of divine authority. I put myself in their place. I feel with them the insistent conviction independent of author's names or method of composition that there is something in these books that is essentially divine. They put a pressure on my conscience and spiritual instinct of the same kind (though not quite in the same degree) as that which the books of Euclid put on my intellect. When I have studied a proposition of Euclid I feel absolutely certain that the conclusion is true—that it must be true—and that not only now and here but in the farthest ages, in the most distant planet. It could never be other than true. Whether the books of Euclid were composed by one man or several, in one year or during centuries, does not affect the position. That is a matter of mere literary interest. The books, however they came, have an inherent impelling power that grips me on the intellectual side. The great utterances of Scripture have a power of the same kind, though from the nature of the case not quite in the same degree, that grips me on my conscience and spiritual side. That is the basis of their authority. That is why the old Jews felt that God was in them. That was why they grew into a Bible.

But for us Christians this conviction has increased a thousandfold by the attitude of the Christ Himself toward this Old Testament. 'It was the Bible of His education. It was the Bible of His ministry. He took for granted its fundamental doctrines about creation, man, righteousness, God's providence and purpose. He accepted it as the preparation for Himself and taught His disciples to find Him in it. He used it to justify His mission and to illumine the mystery of the cross. Above all He fed His own soul with its contents and in the great crises of His life sustained Himself upon it as the solemn word of God.'

This does not mean that He thought its teaching free from all imperfections of its human teachers or that criticism may not have something to teach us of its origin or composition. He criticizes and supersedes some of its precepts. (See Matt. v. 21, 27, 33, 38, 43.) He suggests that it is but a stage toward His own higher teaching. " Ye have heard that it was said by them of old time . . . but I say unto you " something higher still. But whatever its imperfection He certainly gave His full sanction to the belief that the Bible which He loved and studied and used was God's divine authoritative teaching for men. In these days of disquiet about the Old Testament it is surely well to keep that fact in mind.

The New Testament stands in a different position from the Old. For there the central figure is the Son of God Himself. Every word of His was, of course, regarded by His followers as divine, and the Books were accepted because they were believed to tell truly of Him.

Yet as in the case of the Old Testament, the appeal is still to the divine instinct in men. Jesus did not come with compelling external authority, with thunderings and lightnings and the glory of God, forcing men to believe. He came in the form of a carpenter's Son and made His appeal to men's hearts and consciences, as the Old Book had done which testified of Him. And the hearts and consciences of men responded.

This is all we need say here of the position of the New Testament, since the discussion of it comes before us later.

CHAPTER III

CRITICISM AND THE BIBLE

I

Disquiet, and How to Meet it.
BEFORE discussing what modern research has to tell about the making of the Bible, it was necessary for us first to do what we have done—try to understand the impulse which led the Church to make certain books into a Bible, that thus we might realize the solid foundation on which the Bible rests. For if its authority rests not on any external miracle, nor on any author's name, nor on any theory of its composition, nor on any pronouncement of Church or Council or Pope or Saint, but on its own compelling power in every age to convince men that it came from God, then its foundations are safe enough, and the question how the books grew or by whom they were written or edited or brought together into a Bible can be discussed without much

anxiety. It is a secondary matter, a matter of mere literary interest, in no way vital to the authority of the Scriptures.

This is an important point to keep in mind. For during the past century scholars have been discussing as never before, the origins and composition of the Bible. While the discussion was confined to scholars it caused but little trouble. But now that it has come out into the open in sermons and reviews and magazine articles, the Christian public have grown uneasy and perplexed.

"If these scholars are right," they say, "it would seem that the Bible, especially the Old Testament, has not come in the way we thought; that several of the books were not written by the writers nor at the time to which they are usually attributed; that inspired histories instead of being each written by one inspired man have been the result of growth and compiling and editing and revising just like any secular history; that some of the sources are oral traditions floating down in the national memory for centuries; that the Pentateuch as it stands in the Bible to-day appeared first many centuries after the days of Moses. If these things be true they are very startling to us, and our confidence in the Bible is decidedly shaken."

§ 2. No one who has passed through this stage himself can help feeling keen sympathy with faithful hearts disturbed by the intrusion of new thoughts and new view-points.

But these new thoughts and new view-points must be faced. For there is no longer now any serious question as to those disturbing statements just referred to. Whether when rightly read they may not prove the opposite of disturbing is quite another question. But at any rate they are known to be true. There are extreme views and speculations of criticism which are discredited and passing away, but there is no longer any real doubt as to the foundation facts. They have come to stay. The controversy is practically over. Through the laborious investigations of scholars for centuries, God has given new light on the making of the Bible. I believe this new light will bring nobler views of Scripture. But until we have adapted ourselves to it, it is likely to be disquieting.

How shall we adapt ourselves to it? First realize, as has been already said, the solid foundations on which the Bible rests. That is the first important thing to keep in mind when higher criticism disturbs us by upsetting our theories. And this is the second: that we had no business making these theories without any real ground for them, and so perhaps it may be a good thing that somebody should upset them for us. The vague, popular idea is that Moses wrote the first book, the complete Pentateuch; then Joshua wrote the next book and put it beside the first; then Samuel wrote the next, and so on, generation after generation some holy man contributed a completed book and added it to the inspired library of the Jews. It did no harm to believe this so long as nobody knew any reason against it. But when it was questioned we ought to have taken the trouble to find out that it was only an assumption, and that we knew little or nothing about the authorship of the books. Except in the case of the prophets the Old Testament books are all anonymous. The Bible says nothing about their authorship or composition. If we judge the Bible from what it says of itself there is in it no foundation for the popular theory of its origin.

There are some statements on the subject in the Jewish Talmud written in the early Christian centuries, but we have only to read them to see that they are mere conjectures.

Here, for example, is the most famous of them. It is in a Talmud tract, "*Baba Bathra,*" giving certain fanciful reasons as to the order in which the books should stand. Then comes a section on the authorship of the Books—

" And who wrote them (*i.e.* the Books of Scripture) ? Moses wrote his own book, and the section about Balaam and Job. Joshua wrote his own book, and eight verses in the Torah. Samuel wrote his own book and the books of Judges and Ruth. David wrote the book of the Psalms at the direction of the ten elders, the first man, Melchizedek, and Abraham and Moses and Heman and Jeduthun, and Asaph, and the three sons of Korah. Jeremiah wrote his own book, and the book of the Kings and Lamentations. Hezekiah and his company wrote Isaiah, Proverbs, Song of Songs, and Ecclesiastes. The men of the Great Synagogue wrote Ezekiel and the Twelve (minor Prophets), Daniel, and the Roll of Esther. Ezra wrote his own book, and the genealogies in Chronicles down to his own time. . . . Eight verses which are in the Torah Joshua wrote: for the reading is: 'And Moses the servant of the Lord died there.' Is it possible that Moses should have in his lifetime, written the words: 'And he died there'? Was it not that Moses wrote so far and from that point onward Joshua wrote? . . . Joshua wrote his own book: but as for that which is written, 'And Joshua the son of Nun the servant of the Lord died,' Eleazar added it at the end. And whereas it is written, 'And Eleazar the son of Aaron died,' Phinehas and the Elders added that. Whereas it is said Samuel wrote his own book and it is written, 'And Samuel died,' Gad the Seer and Nathan the Prophet added that."

§ 3. Evidently this is all mere conjecture. But such conjectures are responsible for some part at least of the present day vague disquiet. For the early Christian Church in an uncritical age in taking over the Bible of the Jews, took over also some of their theories. By and by these theories grew into the popular Christian tradition, and became so interwoven with men's ideas about the Bible that when scholars began to disturb the theories people got an uneasy feeling they were disturbing the authority of the Bible.

There is a wise saying of Bishop Butler, often quoted, but not so often kept in mind when it is needed.

> "As we are in no sort judges beforehand . . . by what means it were to be expected that God would naturally instruct us, so upon supposition of His affording us light and instruction by Revelation we are in no sort judges by what methods . . . it were to be expected that this supernatural light and instruction would be afforded us. Therefore, neither obscurity . . . nor early disputes about the authors of particular parts, nor any other things of the like kind, though they had been much more considerable than they are could overthrow the authority of Scripture ; unless the Prophets, Apostles, or our Lord had promised that the book containing the Divine Revelation should be secure from such things."

II

The Position To-day. It is hopeful to see how faith and common sense are modifying the position as the years go on. We are gradually adjusting our focus, and getting accustomed to the newer point of view. We see that historical investigation and literary research have raised problems which absolutely necessitate a readjustment of our old conception about the making of the Bible. And the hope is dawning on us that good will come of it. We are remembering how the Evolution scare in the last generation showed the need of readjustment of our views of God and nature, and how through that scare and that readjustment we have greatly gained in our conception of the unsearchable wisdom and goodness of the Creator. And Faith is wispering to us, "It shall be so again. Trust God always. Follow truth at any price and it shall be well." We still see the Word of God exercising continuously its mysterious power on the world. We still see that it came by the operation of the Holy Spirit. But we see that this operation was other than we thought. He left more to human instruments than we once supposed. The beginnings were earlier than our traditions said. Not "Back to Moses," but a millennium before Moses amid a primitive people, amid legends and myths and folk songs "the spirit of God was brooding on the face of the waters," and under His Divine impulse a people and a literature were beginning their rise to the throne of spiritual influence in the world. By strange unnoticed steps, far otherwise than we deemed, the Bible grew, and we, as our first wonder has passed, are beginning to say, "Why not? Why should not God as well reveal Himself in this way as in any other?"

§ 2. And so the Church is settling down again. The odium against criticism is passing away. For it is seen that true and reverent criticism is a handmaid to the Bible, being only the legitimate interpretation of historical facts relating to it. Religion must always gain in the end by the loyal following of truth wherever it leads.

A change has come over the whole spirit of the controversy. There is on the one side more sympathy and more reverence for the Scriptures, and on the other side more generous appreciation of learning and high purpose and long patient work. Also people are less afraid of what may result. They know now the worst that is ever likely to be said. Much of that worst has proved erroneous and passed out of mind. And there is no more such behind. In fact the whole tendency has grown more conservative lately.

§ 3. Now that we are nearing the close of *destructive* criticism—destructive of old theories baseless and untrue, it is surely fitting that the

Church should attempt more, to do *constructive* work, to tell as far as can be known at present the true story of the making of the Bible in the light of modern research. This little book is one—a very humble one—of such efforts on behalf of the thoughtful devout layman who is still puzzled and distressed. Like a child vaguely fearing a bogie in the dark, he does not quite know how much there is to be feared—how much is behind which has not been told to him. Our purpose is to drag out the bogie and show it to him—to tell him frankly the disturbing things that have been learned that he may judge for himself if he has reason to be afraid of them.

To many who have thought very deeply about it, it seems that the Bible will be the richer for all that we have learned—that its inspiration will be more understood and appreciated as we realize more, in the fuller light of historical research, the tender and wonderful methods of God's self-revelation to man, His patience and resourcefulness and silent workings unseen by any human eye.

PART II
THE MAKING OF THE OLD TESTAMENT

CHAPTER I

THE LOST LIBRARY

The First Stage in Bible-making.
WITH this preparation we proceed to tell briefly of the making of the Old Testament, which differs only in this from the making of the New, that while the New Testament was completed in one generation, the Old Testament was in the making for nearly 2000 years.

The story, as we have already said, is in two stages :

First. THE FORMATION OF A RELIGIOUS LITERATURE. How it was composed, what earlier sources were used, how far the books may have been combined and worked over and edited and revised.

Second. THE SELECTION OR ACCEPTANCE OR RECOGNITION OF CERTAIN PARTS OF THIS LITERATURE —the process by which certain books impressed themselves on the national consciousness as being especially inspired of God, so that the Jewish Church was led to place them apart from its other literature as divine and authoritative, and so to collect them into a Jewish Bible.

§ 2. We begin with the first. Does any reader think that the Old Testament began with the books which are in our hands to-day? A very little study of its structure will dissipate that idea. The Bible itself distinctly contradicts it. Long before a chapter of our Bible was written there existed an older religious literature now lost for ever which seems to have been quite familiar to the writers of Scripture.

This is what any thoughtful scholar would naturally expect. He sees even in the oldest books of our present Scriptures a finished literary style and an appeal to a previous religious knowledge on the reader's part, which at once makes him feel that there must have been earlier literary compositions and earlier religious teaching for some considerable time before. That this was so we gather from the Old Testament writers themselves.

They tell us in the Pentateuch that they went to their "Book of the Wars of Jehovah" for the Song of the Arnon valleys (Num. xxi. 14), they quote the Song of the Well from the folk-songs of their day

(Numb. xxi. 17, 18), the Book of Jasher was their source for the battle of Bethoron and the sun standing still (Josh. x. 10). Later on they turn up this same Book of Jasher for the Song of the Bow, the lament over Saul and Jonathan (2 Sam. i. 18) and other incidents are quoted freely from the Book of Nathan, the Book of Gad, the Book of Jehu, the Book of Shemaiah, the Book of Iddo the Seer, etc.

Which at once sets us wondering about this ancient lost literature from which these books were picked out for quotation. What was the extent of it? What were the contents? How far did it go back? How much of still earlier literature was incorporated in it—songs, perhaps, and legends and thoughts and guesses of the prehistoric days when the world was young?

It is a question of mere literary interest, but surely of enthralling literary interest What and where were the beginnings of the Bible, the ultimate, far back, very first beginnings of elements afterwards built into the structure of the Old Testament?

§ 3. How can we know anything about it, some one asks, since we have no history to tell us? Neither has the scientist, we reply, who seeks to learn the story of the making of the mountains. We can but do what he does. As the geologist digs into the strata of the rocks for traces of the old-world shells and animal remains which compose them, so we can dig into the strata of the Old Testament, seeking traces of the old-world literature built into it. And in doing so we find exciting answers to our guesses ; we are brought back to the child races of the world, to the beginnings of the Jewish Church to the laws and legends of a primitive people, to the rude ballads and war songs and histories of far-back days when bards and story-tellers took the place of books, and history was transmitted by word of mouth.

Thus began the early literature of every people. Thus began the early literature of the Jews. Thus began the making of the Bible.

It was not " Bible " yet ; it was only amongst the "*origines,*" the beginnings. But we believe that God was behind these little beginnings as He is behind the little rivulets where the rivers rise. I am writing this on the banks of the lower St. Lawrence, twelve miles wide as it draws toward the sea. Behind it lie the Great Lakes, and behind these the many rivers of the West, and farther back the mountain torrents and the rivulets which feed them, and behind these the drainage of the far-away hills, and behind all, the rain from heaven. We must get back there to complete the illustration. It was the rain from heaven that began the mighty river. It was God who helped the thoughts and questionings of the child races of earth which after many generations touched the making of the Bible.

§ 4. The world would give a good deal to-day for the recovery of that ancient lore which inspiration caught up afterwards and brought into the Bible. Possibly the explorer's spade may yet find parts of it as it has found much older matter. But in all probability it is lost to us for ever, except what men have been able to discover in the Bible.

Later on we shall examine their methods of discovery and watch men digging not into the earth but into the strata of the Bible to uncover the old literature embedded there in ancient days. It seems unwise to do it here lest it should break the connection of thought. Meantime it will be convenient here to indicate what traces they have found. Here is a rough list, partly conjectural, but mainly resting on definite evidence in the Scriptures—a list or which the bulk of modern scholars would agree:

Ancient Lore. **The old Semitic Legends of the Creation and the Deluge** from the cradle of the Hebrew race, not in their crude pagan form but purified and transfigured after contact for centuries with the religious life of Israel.

Ballads and Folksongs of earliest days sung around the camp fires and in the tribal gatherings.

Oral histories of great deeds of the past told by the story-tellers at feast and festival.

Cuneiform Inscriptions on Tiles, the probable originals, e.g. of Gen. xiv., etc.

Cycles of Legends of the Patriarchs current amongst the people and preserved at the sanctuaries connected with their names—Shechem and Bethel and Shiloh and Mahanaim.

Codes of ancient laws, oral or written, originating with Moses, amongst them the Book of the Covenant, the Law of Holiness, etc., and prominent above all, the Ten Commandments.

Stories of the Exodus. Written records of the desert journeys. Directions about worship. Teachings of Moses.

The Ballads and histories of the Judges preserved at their several centres. **Songs and Camp Stories** about Saul and David, etc.

Records of the schools of the prophets, from Samuel to Elijah. **Historical notes** by the official recorders.

Collections. **The Book of the Wars of Jehovah. The Book of Jasher. The Book of Nathan. The Book of Gad. The Book of Iddo the Seer. The Book of Jehu. The Book of Shemaiah. The Acts of Solomon. The Chronicles of the kings of Judah. The Chronicles of Israel.**

Sheets of Psalms from the temple choir desks. **Collection of Proverbs** by the men of Hezekiah and others (Prov. xxv. 1). **The sermons and predictions of the prophets,** some of which were written down by the prophets or their disciples.

Bibles before the Bible. **The Bible of Southern Judah,** (the Jahvist Bible, ninth century B.C.), **The Bible of Northern Israel** (the Elohist Bible, eighth century B.C.), **The Book of Deuteronomy,** 621 B.C., **The Book of the Priests.**

This is all that we can find of the lost sacred literature which was extant in the days of the prophets and kings. What the whole extent of it was no man can tell. It was not "Bible." We cannot yet assume the thought of a Bible. The need had not yet come. Religion was kept alive for Israel by the worship of Jehovah, by the oral teaching of the priests, by the inspired utterances of the prophets. They did not need a Bible.

But the idea of a Bible had already taken root and was growing. Doubtless the Ten Commandments were venerated as divine. The Book of the Covenant and the Law of Holiness stood prominent amongst the laws. Later we shall see the reverence for Deuteronomy, and we know that the prophets' sermons were regarded as inspired. Here, already, was the essential idea of a Bible. And surely we are not wrong in thinking that a Divine Providence was guiding the writers of the old history and literature, that unconscious preparation for the Bible that was to be.

CHAPTER II

SOME CONTENTS OF THE LOST LIBRARY

I

The Creation and Deluge Legends. Now we are to seek for ourselves in the Bible, traces of this old lost literature, by methods which are explained in a later chapter. And at the very first step—in the very first chapters of Genesis—straightway we are carried back to the old-world days, to the infancy of the Hebrew race, when Abram came wandering out of Ur of the Chaldees, one thousand years before Moses. For there in the twilight of history in the cradle of the Hebrew race, there were around him prehistoric legends of the Creation and the Flood. We have found them and can read them to-day. Abram and the men of his time must have known them. And if so, they must have remembered them. 'God did not obliterate the whole contents of the religious consciousness of the Abrahamic family when he called Abraham to leave his country.' These legends were primitive, childish, almost grotesque in parts, and they clearly belonged to a people who believed in many gods. That is perfectly natural, just what we should expect in those old Semitic races from which Israel sprang, when " their fathers dwelt of old time beyond the River, even Terah, the father of Abraham and the father of Nahor, and they served other gods " (Josh. xxiv. 2). They were blind guesses of the old child-races long ago, puzzling in wonder and awe over the mystery of Creation—blind guesses about a Creator—may we not say blind gropings after God? At first sight we should feel sure that they could never touch the Bible. But it is hard to judge beforehand what may or may not happen in the mysterious working of God's Providence. At any rate, if we are seeking truth we must face the facts before us. There are such reminiscences of them in the great epics of Genesis that we cannot escape the feeling that there must be some connection.

§ 2. In 1853, Hormuzd Rassam, assistant to Sir Henry Layard, was exploring the buried ruins of Nineveh and Nimrud (note the name Nimrud, Gen. x. 10, and the name Erech on p. 52). There he came on the large collection of clay tablets forming the library of Assurbanipal, King of Nineveh, which he at once sent on to the British Museum to await deciphering. In these were afterwards found the now famous Creation and Deluge tablets.

The Creation tablets tell a story too long and complicated to give here in detail. The main thought is that in the beginning was chaos without form and void, from which sprang the gods. Their resolve to create a world leads to a mighty conflict between Marduk (Merodach, Jer. l. 2) the sun god, the god of Creation, and Tiamat the great Deep—the mighty dragon of the slime. Marduk cleaves the dragon in two (see probably a curious reminiscence in Isa. li. 9, "Art not thou he who wounded the Dragon?"). From one half he makes the firmament to keep the upper waters ("the waters above the firmament" in Genesis); from the other half he makes the earth. Then he made the sun and the stars.

"He caused the moon god to shine forth and entrusted to him the night,
Appointed him as a nightbody to determine the days."

Then came plants and animals, and lastly man—

"He opened his mouth and to Ea (he spake)
'My blood will I take and bone will I (fashion)
I will make man that man may . . .
I will create man who shall inhabit (the earth?)
That the service of the gods may be established and their shrines . . .'"

§ 3. The resemblance is much more evident in the Deluge legend. In 1872, George Smith, the famous Assyrian investigator, was working in the British Museum over the tile inscriptions unearthed by Rassam in the Nineveh Palace Library. Amongst them he found the twelve tablets of the Epic of King Gilgamesh, telling the adventures of that mighty hunter the hero of Uruk (compare Nimrod the builder of Erech (Uruk), Gen. x. 10) in his search after immortality. Scholars date it back to about 2000 B.C. The 11th tablet (see photograph) contains a Deluge story. It tells that in the city of Surripak on the Euphrates the gods resolved to bring about a flood. Their resolve was communicated to Hasisadra. The gods bade him build a ship whose height should be 120 cubits, and its breadth 120 cubits, and take refuge in it with his family and slaves and stores for subsistence; also to bring in cattle and beasts of the earth to keep seed alive on the earth. He built the ship as directed, and pitched it within and without. Then he entered in and closed the door. Then came the awful storm and flood at which the gods in heaven were frightened and wept. The flood lasted six days, and he watched the corpses floating by. On the seventh day it began to subside, and after seven days more the ship

FRAGMENTS OF THE DELUGE TABLETS
The Eleventh Tablet of the Epic of Gilgamesh containing the Deluge Story.

rested on the mountains of Nizir. Then the poem goes on—

> "When the seventh day arrived
> I brought out a dove and let it go
> The dove went to and fro
> As there was no resting place it turned back
> I brought forth a swallow and let it go
> As there was no resting-place it turned back
> I brought forth a raven and let it go
> The raven went forth and saw the decrease of the waters
> It ate, it waded, it croaked it turned not back.
> Then I sent forth, everything to the four winds
>   I offered sacrifice
> The gods smelt the savour
> The gods smelt the goodly savour [1]
> The gods gathered like flies over the sacrifice."

* * * *

Then he tells how the goddess Istar lighted up the rainbow, and how the gods pleaded that all should not be destroyed, only the sinners, not the righteous, etc.

§ 4. Now when we find poems such as these coming down, it is believed, from Abram's day and from the birthplace of the Hebrew race, and when we notice their curious coincidences with the Genesis story, it cannot but set us thinking. It hardly seems unreasonable to suppose that they represent

---

[1] Compare Gen. viii. 21, " The Lord smelled the sweet savour."

a version of some widespread Creation and Deluge legends among the peoples from whom Israel sprang; or to wonder if they have not some relation to our Bible.

It seems startling to connect the noble stories in Genesis with these grotesque legends, yet the evidence certainly points that way. That there is some connection is beyond question. The earlier cannot be a corruption of the later. That both should have sprung from an earlier common source does not help us, for that common source in those pagan days would differ little from that which we have found. All probability points to the theory in which most modern scholars are now agreed, that the early wandering shepherds of the Hebrews were familiar with the notions of the race from which they came, that these old legends floated down for centuries in the folklore of primitive Israel, that mingling with the stream of thought of a people impressed by the presence of a holy God, the polytheism and degrading ideas could not remain. The Spirit of God was moving on the face of the waters, working, as it is the economy of the Divine method to work, upon existing materials. Priest and prophet and pious parent would tell the old story in the light of their religious knowledge. And so while their form remained the old legends were transfigured. Passing through the crucible of faithful souls a Divine touch and yet a Diviner touch was added as they came down through the years, till the simple child story of many gods with human passions became the story of the one God holy and just Who made the sun and moon which the Chaldeans worshipped and the great bulls to which the Egyptians prayed, and as the crown and summit of His work made man in His image after His likeness; till the legend of Paradise was touched by inspiration to become a vehicle of deepest spiritual truth, of the rise of conscience, of the coming of evil, of the dread which every man feels in his secret sin, when he hears the voice of the Lord God in the garden in the cool of the day and is afraid and hides himself. Where the Babylonian poet saw only the action of deified forces of nature the Hebrew writer saw the working of God. And that insight was Inspiration.

Then when priests and prophets divinely guided began to write their elementary Bibles (see next chapter) naturally they would think of beginning at the Creation. I picture to myself such a writer meditating on those purified creation stories of his people, till they emerged from his hand in that prose poem which has come down to us from the Bible of the Priests, "IN THE BEGINNING GOD CREATED THE HEAVENS AND THE EARTH."

True, this is only a conjecture. But the conjecture has strong facts behind it. And if it be so it need in no wise disturb our faith. If things so happened it was surely by Divine inspiration. If the vague thoughts of the old child races were thus cleansed from their corruption, it was surely the Spirit of God that cleansed them, and "what God hath cleansed that call not thou common." Therefore none the less we regard the story as inspired in the form in which it has come to us, the form "which it received from devout Israelites moved by the Spirit of God and penetrated with the belief in the spiritual Jehovah. By saints and prophets it was purified and hallowed that it might subserve the divine purpose of transmitting as in a figure to future generations spiritual teaching on eternal truths.[1]

II

The Age of Song and Story.

In our Lost Library was much of ancient song and story.

There is no doubt that the ultimate beginnings of Bible history and literature were mainly oral, ballads and folk songs recited among the people; stories of the distant past told

[1] Ryle, "Early Narratives of Genesis."

in shepherds' watches and around the camp fires, and afterwards collected in groups in literary form; laws and judgments, some of them written, most of them handed down orally for generations by the priests at the various sanctuaries.

The literature of almost every nation begins with easy alliterative verse, songs of famous men and famous deeds sung by the people in the early days when writing was not known or the people could not read. It seems to have been especially so in Israel. Most of the direct quotations from ancient sources are in verse, and are so printed in the English Revised Version. The way in which they are introduced suggests that they usually represent the older original sources used by the Bible writers which, by the way, may be the explanation of the poetical rhythm in much of our Old Testament prose.

We can almost see the writer using his originals. They are apparently in poetry, which he is condensing into a prose story. But sometimes his poetical instinct is too strong for him, and he gives us delightful little glimpses of the sources before him by lifting direct into his book a bit of the historic song which is running in his head or which is written in his ancient manuscripts, and so enables us to reproduce in part the primitive "song and story literature."

§ 2. Here are some of the extracts, amongst them being a couple of pages copied direct from the Book of Jasher and one extract, at least, from the Book of the Wars of Jehovah.

This is now bone of my bone
And flesh of my flesh
This one shall be called Woman
For from Man was she taken.

• • • •

Cursed shalt thou be above all animals
And above all the beasts of the earth
On thy belly shalt thou go
And dust shalt thou eat.

• • • •

Adah and Zillah hearken to my voice
Wives of Lamech give ear unto my saying
For I have slain a man for wounding me
And a young man for bruising me
If Cain shall be avenged sevenfold
Lamech shall be seventy and seven.

• • • •

Blessed of Jehovah be Shem
Let Canaan be a servant unto him
    God enlarge Japhet!
Let him dwell in the tents of Shem
Let Canaan be a servant unto him.

• • • •

Two nations are in thy womb
Two peoples shall be separated from thy bowels
The one people shall be stronger than the other
And the elder shall serve the younger.

• • • •

May God give thee of the dew of Heaven
And of the fatness of the earth
And plenty of corn and wine
Let peoples serve thee
And nations bow down to thee
Be lord over thy brethren
And let thy mother's sons bow down to thee
Cursed be every one that curseth thee
And blessed be every one that blesseth thee.

   * * * *

Assemble yourselves and hear ye sons of Jacob
And hearken unto Israel your father
Reuben thou art my firstborn.

(Etc., etc., a poem of twenty-seven verses.)

   * * * *

I will sing unto Jehovah for he hath triumphed
 gloriously
The horse and his rider hath he cast into the sea
Jehovah is my strength and my song
And is become my salvation
Jehovah is a man of war
Jehovah is his name

(Etc., etc., a poem of eighteen verses.)

And Miriam answered them—

Sing ye to the Lord for he hath triumphed gloriously
The horse and his rider hath he cast into the sea.

   * * * *

Vaheb in Suphah
 And the valleys of Arnon
 And the slope of the valleys
  That inclineth towards Ar.

(Copied from the Book of the Wars of Jehovah to insert in Numb. xxi.)

From Aram hath Balak brought me
The King of Moab from the mountains of the east
    Come curse me Jacob
    Come defy me Israel.

   (Etc., etc. Three extracts from the Song of Balaam.)

    •   •   •   •

Sun stand thou still upon Gibeon,
And thou moon in the valley of Ajalon.
And the sun stood still and the moon stayed
Until the nation had avenged themselves of their enemies.

   (Copied from the Book of Jasher to insert in Josh. x.)

    •   •   •   •

Awake, awake, Deborah!
Awake, awake, utter a song!
Arise, Barak! Lead captivity captive.

The river of Kishon swept them away
That ancient river, the river of Kishon
Then did the horse hoofs stamp
With the pransings, the pransings of the mighty ones.

    •   •   •   •

Blessed above woman shall Jael be
The wife of Heber the Kenite
Water he asked, milk she gave
Curdled milk in a lordly dish
She put her hand to the nail
And her right hand to the workman's hammer
Yea she pierced and struck through his temples
At her feet he bowed, he fell, he lay down
At her feet he bowed, he fell
Where he bowed there he fell down dead.

    •   •   •   •

Through the window she peered and loudly cried
The mother of Sisera through the lattice

Why is his chariot so long in coming?
Why delay the clatter of the hoofs of his horses?
The wisest of her ladies answered her
Yea she answered her own question
"Are they not finding, dividing the spoil
A damsel or two for each of the men
For Sisera a spoil of dyed stuffs
A spoil of dyed stuffs embroidered
A piece or two of embroidery for his neck."

. . . . .

So let all thine enemies perish, O Jehovah
But they who love him shall be as the sun in invincible splendour.

. . . .

> Thy glory O Israel is slain in thy high places
> How are the mighty fallen!
> Tell it not in Gath
>   Publish it not in the streets of Askalon
> Lest the daughters of the Philistines rejoice
> Lest the daughters of the uncircumcised triumph.
>
>   (Etc., etc.)

(This "Song of the Bow" was first taught orally to the people and afterwards preserved in the Book of Jasher, from which it was copied for use in 2 Sam. i.)

All this gives us a glimpse of the way in which, by means of verse, history was transmitted orally from generation to generation. But this does not by any means indicate the amount of poetical composition. All the prophecies before the Exile were poems and the majority of those later. Job is a great dramatic poem. The deeds of national heroes were commemorated in verse, the conqueror came from battle to the sound of singing, " Saul hath slain his thousands and David his ten thousands " (1 Sam. xviii. 7). The digging of the well of Heshbon is celebrated in a ballad (Num. xxi. 17). There are harvest songs and drinking songs and wedding and love songs (see an exquisite collection in the Book of Canticles). The Book of Jasher seems to have been such a ballad collection, as also the " Book of the Wars of Jehovah."

§ 3. Ballad history has the advantage of being easily remembered and transmitted, and also of being less liable than prose to changes in transmission. And beside the ballads would run the stream of oral tradition ; the legends of the patriarchs which gathered round their chief centres Shechem and Hebron and Bethel and Shiloh ; the stories told in the lonely pastures " when shepherds watched their flocks by night," or recited by practised story-tellers at the feasts and tribal gatherings. We must put ourselves in their place to realize the position. Picture the crowds going up to worship at any of the sanctuaries, and hearing every time its patriarchal legends. Picture the village girls in the evening at the well loitering over the tale of the Wooing of Rebecca; and the rude rough shepherds laughing in their delight over the oft-told story of Samson tricking the stupid Philistines.

Thus would the common people learn the brave deeds of old, sometimes lightly in heedless mood, sometimes more seriously as the thought of God came in, in His dealings with Jacob, in the deeds of the Judges, in the solemn days when Moses led their fathers through the Wilderness.

This is a common phenomenon of life to-day in the unchanging East. Eastern history mainly springs from such sources. We can hardly be wrong in transferring it to those older days. Life was dull; there were no newspapers or books. There was not much to talk of. So the old stories would be greatly prized and memory with no books to lean on could perform feats impossible to us, and carry on history through many generations.

III

The Lives of the Patriarchs. In this way must have been transmitted the story of the Patriarchs. The first written record we have is in the "Northern and Southern Bibles" (Elohist and Jahvist, see next chapter), about the ninth or tenth century B.C. There is no reason to doubt that they got it from earlier sources, oral or written, in the same way as they tell us they got the rest of their history, and these sources in turn must have gone back to still earlier times. These Northern and Southern versions of the story vary somewhat from each other much as the Four Gospels do, or as any story might be expected to do when transmitted through different channels. But in the main they corroborate each other. All this points to a real story of real people come down through the separate traditions of the North and South.

§ 2. It is difficult to understand its oral transmission through so long an interval. Probably there were written records. Writing was well known even in Abram's day. But it is only fair to say we have no hint of such, and we notice that while these " bibles " tell repeatedly of written authorities for certain parts of their Mosaic history (Exod. xvii. 14, xxiv. 4, 7 ; Num. xxxiii. 2, xxi. 14 ; Deut. xxxi. 9 ; Josh. x. 13), no such authorities are quoted for the Genesis narrative. If there were none then it must have come by oral tradition through the age of song and story in Israel's early life. It must be so unless it was all pure invention. And even judging the Bible by the rules of ordinary secular history, that is a solution which no serious scholar would accept for a moment. For it would raise far greater difficulties than that of the oral transmission. Surely it would be a stretch of credulity to believe that a history which has so grown into the life and literature of Israel has no reality behind it, merely because it is difficult to explain how it came down. Why, the whole history of Israel would have to be rewritten from the beginning if we had to leave out the patriarchs. All over it in every age, in song and story and history and prophecy, are the traces of them. Everywhere it is assumed that Jehovah their God is the God of their fathers, the God of Abraham and Isaac and Jacob. How could this be accounted for unless it were true? Why should Israel carry back its history at all behind Moses their Founder if that history were not already existing? And if one should suppose that they invented it, why should any proud people invent such a discreditable story telling of their degrading origin as slaves—telling of their holy ancestor Abraham lying shamefully and repeatedly about his wife—of Israel, whose name they bore, cheating his old blind father; of Judah, the head of a great tribe, sinning with Tamar the Canaanitess; of Reuben, committing incest with his father's concubine? Nations do not usually invent stories such as those about their past. And how did Moses come to the slaves in Egypt, assuming their knowledge of such past history? The mission of Moses is hardly intelligible except there was some previous religious preparation. The whole Exodus history declares that he did not proclaim any unknown God or any new religion. The story enshrined in the national memory makes it all simple and intelligible. " The God of your fathers hath sent me to you, the God of Abraham and Isaac and Jacob."

§ 3. It has been suggested that the Patriarchal story may be perhaps a history of personified tribes, a sort of parable story, Abraham, Isaac, and Jacob being the names of clans, marriage signifying the union of clans, death the extinction of a clan, etc. Such legends have appeared in the traditions of other nations. But there seems no basis for such a theory beyond the bare fact that Israel is often called by the name of its great ancestor. No one ever heard of a tribe or people called Abram or Isaac, while the names are common in ancient days as personal names. Possibly the tribal histories affected the stories in their transmission, but they are certainly no mere stories of personified tribes. Let any one try to read the story in Genesis as a historical parable, and see how hopeless is the attempt. Then read it as a simple tale of real flesh-and-blood men following their ordinary avocations, working and travelling and loving and suffering and sinning and struggling in their poor way after God and Right—and it must be evident that the narrators were depicting ordinary life and that the first written histories were recording traditions enshrined in the national consciousness generation after generation.

§ 4. Perhaps we are exaggerating the difficulty of such long oral transmission in days when nearly all history had to be transmitted orally and memory in consequence was more highly tenacious, especially in the case of great national events or great national celebrities. I have just met with a striking instance of two men carrying the tradition of a special occurrence connected with Yale College over a space of 172 years. It happened when the first was a boy eight years of age, and when he was an old man the other as a young student heard him tell it in public.[1] There are many instances recorded

[1] Gregory, "Canon and Text of New Testament," p. 161.

where a succession of four or five men have carried on a tradition for centuries.

Assuming the story of the Patriarchs to be substantially true these ancestors of the race were very conspicuous men in the eyes of their descendants. The lives of Abraham, Isaac, and Jacob would be well known to Joseph and his brethren. A race of men in Egyptian slavery would be likely to cherish the stories of the past, especially if they contained promises of good days to come. The great crises of the Exodus suggesting a fulfilment of such hopes might well deepen and intensify the memory of the old traditions. If, as many scholars believe, part of the Hebrew race never went to Egypt, but remained still in Canaan, these traditions might also be preserved in the chief centres of the Patriarchs' lives in that land.

We can only conjecture. There are difficulties about these far-reaching traditions, but there can be no serious question that they had substantial historical facts behind them. Therefore we unhesitatingly place them in that long lost lore which existed for many centuries before the Bible.

§ 5. We must freely recognize that after many centuries of oral transmission we cannot feel confident of accuracy in details. Bards and story-tellers were likely in some degree to idealize their heroes. Stories might grow and be altered in transmission. Probably confusion would sometimes arise, as in cases where a similar story is told of Abraham and of Isaac (cf. Gen. xii. and xxvi.). Let all this be granted to the full. But this does not affect the substantial truth of the story or bid us doubt that we are dealing with traditions of real men and women current in some form from very early days.

Let imagination conjure up those early days and the primitive child race which thus learned its religion. What conjectures and emotions it sets stirring in one's mind! Was the Providence of God protecting these old legends? Did the slaves in Egypt tell them to each other? Was this the religious knowledge which made Joseph such a hero? Did Moses' mother teach it to her boy when she nursed him in the palace of Pharaoh's daughter? How otherwise did Moses begin to learn about Jehovah? Was this part of the thought in the inspired writer's mind when he tells that "God Who spake to the fathers in many times and in many manners hath in these last days spoken unto us by His Son"?

IV

The Mosaic Writings. In our Lost Library were also, as we shall see later, the sources of the Pentateuch laws and Mosaic history. We are assuming here the conclusion in which now practically all scholars are agreed that the Pentateuch as it stands to-day is a compilation from earlier sources, a completed edition of the story of Moses and of various collections of laws whose origin and nucleus go back to Moses' day.

In our Lost Library then, say about the time of King David, we should find not our completed Pentateuch but separate sources of it, such as the Ten Commandments, the Book of the Covenant (Exod. xx. to xxiii.), the Law of Holiness (Lev. xvii. to xxvi.), the history of Battles, the itinerary of the Wanderings, codes of Laws, some of them written, some of them existing orally in the several sanctuaries in the memories of the priests who dispensed justice.

Later on we shall find collections of this material, in the Northern and Southern Bibles, and in the Bible of the Priests. The writers of course got their matter from the earlier sources existing in their day, some of it oral, certainly some of it written, and amongst these written sources some which, at least in their opinion, had come from the hand of Moses himself. They tell us that " Moses wrote in a book" the Battle with Amalek (Exod. xvii. 14), and the Desert Journeys (Num. xxxiii. 2), and the Book of the Covenant (Exod. xx. to xxiii., see Exod. xxiv. 4-7), and other collections of laws (Exod. xxiv. 7; xxxiv. 27). Apparently they knew these books, or knew about them, and believed Moses to be the author. Even if they were mistaken in that opinion it is evident at any rate that there were about the ninth or tenth century B.C. some written books so ancient that they could be attributed to Moses.

§ 2. For our belief in inspiration and in the Divine guidance of Moses and the Jewish Church, it is not at all necessary to think that every jot and tittle of the laws in the Pentateuch came from Moses himself. The laws of Solon in Athens, the laws of Moses, the psalms of David, the proverbs of Solomon would naturally take the name of the man who originated them. All the evidence points to the belief that the great leader gave his people judgments and laws which were at least the nucleus of the future codes. But it is evident that change of time and circumstances necessitated additions to these, which were added of course by his successors.

We have most interesting glimpses of the growth of the laws. Moses is sitting to judge the people from morning till evening. " I judge," he says to his father-in-law, " between a man and his neighbour, and I make them know the statutes of God and His laws " (Exod. xviii. 16). Then Jethro advises the appointment of subordinate judges who would have to be guided in their decisions by some simple laws. Long afterwards we find Deborah under the palm tree at Lapidoth, where the people came to her for judgment (Judges iv. 5), and Samuel going in circuit to Bethel and Gilgal and Mizpah, and he judged Israel in all these places (1 Sam. vii. 17).

Thus decisions would naturally be generalized and codes of law would grow and the judges would feel that they were under the guidance of God.

There seems no reason either why Moses or his successors should not have adapted to their purpose some good laws already existing in the civilized countries around. In fact, we know that they did so. The French excavators at Susa in 1901 came on a most interesting find—the laws of the Babylonian King Hammurabi (supposed to be the Amraphel of Gen. xiv.) written on a great stone block and belonging probably to about 2150 B.C. (about the time of Abraham) (see photograph). Compare some of its sections with the " Book of the Covenant," which is considered to be amongst the oldest part of the laws in the Pentateuch:—

[Photograph by Mansell & Co.

THE BLACK DIORITE BLOCK
Found in Susa 1901, representing King Hammurabi receiving the Laws from his God.

HAMMURABI.

§§ 196, 200. If a man hath caused the loss of another's eye then some one shall cause his eye to be lost. If he hath broken another's limb (or tooth) some one shall break his limb (or tooth).

§§ 199, 201. If he hath caused the loss of the eye or limb of a man's servant, then shall he pay half his price. If he hath caused the loss of a tooth of a freed slave, then shall he pay one third of a mina of silver.

§ 250. If a savage ox in his charge hath gored a man and caused him to die, then that case hath no recompense.

§ 251. But if the goring ox hath made known his vice that he gores and the owner hath not blunted his horns or secured the ox, and this ox gores and slays a freeborn man, then his owner shall pay . . .

§ 252. If it gore a man's servant, the owner shall pay one-third of a mina of silver.

§ 125. If a man hath placed anything on deposit and something hath been lost the owner of the house shall make good and then seek out and recover it from the thief.

EXODUS.

xxi. 22. If any mischief follow then thou shalt give life for life, eye for eye, tooth for tooth, hand for hand, foot for foot.

xxi. 26. If a man smite the eye (or tooth) of his servant or of his maid and destroy it, then shall he let him go for his eye's (or tooth's) sake.

xxi. 28, 29. If an ox gore a man or woman that they die, the owner of the ox shall be quit. But if the ox were wont to gore in time past, and it hath been testified to the owner, and he hath not kept him in, but that he hath killed a man or woman, then shall the ox be stoned, and the owner put to death.

xxi. 32. If the ox gore a servant he shall give unto their master thirty shekels of silver, and the ox shall be stoned.

xxii. 7. If a man shall deliver unto his neighbour money or stuff to keep, and it be stolen out of the man's house, if the thief be found, he shall pay double.

F

What does this show? That the wise old lawgiver and his successors had the good sense to use or modify and incorporate in their code, laws which had proved their value among other peoples. "Grant us," says the Whitsuntide collect, "Grant us by the same Spirit to have a right judgment in all things." This right judgment which Israel's lawgivers used is surely one of the fruits of the Spirit. If any man should think that the only possible inspiration would be a mechanical dictating of every law by the Holy Spirit to Moses, then he has simply got to correct his views of inspiration. The facts do not fit them.

V

The Rest of the Religious Literature. As the years went on, through the Providence of God, all unconsciously men were gathering and preserving material for the Bible that was to be. The ballads and poems grew into collections like the Book of Jasher. The legends were brought together in connected cycles and put in literary form. From the School of the Prophets came the vivid story of Elijah and his compeers, and doubtless very much more of such history besides. In the various sanctuaries priests gathered their laws and oral traditions. There were historical notes by the official Recorders (2 Sam. viii. 16; 1 Kings iv. 3, etc.). Many of the earliest prophets were writers of books, a tantalizing list that we can never now examine, the Books of Nathan and Gad and Jehu and Iddo the Seer and Shemaiah and the rest.

Then there were the collections of Proverbs by the men of Hezekiah and others (Prov. xxv. 1). There were psalms and sacred lyrics in the First Temple, and amongst the people. (No critic can persuade us that this poetry-loving Israel reserved its songs of praise till the days of the Exile.) And last, but not least, came the Sermons of the Great Prophets, which were one day to stand out so prominently in the Bible.

Be it remembered that all this material was not yet regarded as " Bible " in our sense of the word. It was simply the religious literature of ancient Israel.

CHAPTER III

THE "BIBLES BEFORE THE BIBLE"

I

How Prophets wrote History. Now that we have found so much of the material for the Old Testament, let us get on with the making.

So far as we can judge this making proceeded gradually. First came written collections of the old ballads and legends, such as the Book of Jasher, the Book of the Upright, probably a book of heroic ballads about the great men of the past—and the Book of the Wars of Jehovah, a collection of many story-tellers' narratives of the brave days of old. There were probably several such collections now lost to us for ever.

Then came earnest prophets and teachers touched by the Spirit of Jehovah, teaching and illustrating from the story of the past great lessons of God and Life and Duty. They were not so much concerned with the details of the history as with its solemn lessons. They selected what they wanted to illustrate their themes. They left out what they did not want. They would certainly not be regarded in our day as scientific historians. But it might be good for us if more of their spirit were in our histories to-day.

Take for example the collection of legends of the Judges which grew up at the several centres where they lived. Then see the inspired prophet writer taking these stories and placing them in the setting suitable for his purpose. See his continually recurring formulæ—

The children of Israel sinned against the Lord,
And the Lord sold them into the hand of . . .
Then the children of Israel cried unto the Lord,
And the Lord raised up unto them a deliverer.

That is the setting or framework of his pictures. The whole story is told in a continuous cycle of sinning and suffering and repenting and deliverance and sinning again and suffering and repenting and deliverance, and behind it all is a loving holy God. It is the inspired writer's view of the philosophy of history. He is not content with the outward phenomena. He wants "to see the wheels go round." And to him God is behind the wheels. That is where his inspiration comes in.

Is not that mainly where our English history

differs from that of the ancient Jews? Surely God is behind our history too. In the days of the Armada we openly said so. But our historians do not look much for Him. They show us the outward happenings. They show us, as it were, a closed clock, and trace the movements of the hands. The old prophets showed a skeleton clock with the springs and wheels in sight. Perhaps they did not always explain the movements truly. But they tried.

In this spirit doubtless was written the old lost books of Gad and Iddo the Seer, and Shemaiah and the rest of them. In this spirit were written other and more important sacred histories which we have now to tell of—" Bibles before the Bible," I call them—which were afterwards worked in in the making of the Pentateuch. They belong to the Lost Library, but we have recovered parts of them. First of them comes the bible of Southern Judah, the Jahvist Bible.

I

The Bible of Southern Judah.

It came to pass in the days of the prophet Elijah that God raised up another prophet far greater than he—not for preaching to crowds nor for striving with kings, but for greater and more enduring work. A scholar, a historian, a literary artist, a man deeply touched by the Spirit of Jehovah, he took for his great life task the making of a Bible that Israel might know the Lord. No man knows the name or the habitation of this silent worker. But his work remains his monument for ever.

I picture him in his workroom in the city of Jerusalem, or away amid the hills in the School of the Prophets. Centuries of religious teaching lie behind him. He is familiar with the great national traditions current in his day. He and his disciples have collected books of our " Lost Library." They have gathered cycles of legends from the several sanctuaries; stories of Jacob, which clustered around Bethel and Shiloh and Mahanaim; stories of Isaac from Beersheba; of Abram from Shechem and Hebron and of other sacred places; histories both oral and written of the great days of Moses specially cherished for centuries in the memories of the people. Codes of laws were of course the easiest to obtain, since they were in common use in the administering of justice.

But our silent old prophet does not trouble much with laws, it is the history that stirs his blood. His attitude is that of the Church in her litany, " O God, we have heard with our ears and our fathers have declared to us the noble works that thou didst in their days, and in the old time before them." He is no mere collector, no mere dry historian. He is an enthusiast. He is also a great literary as well as spiritual genius. By frequent dialogues and picturesque vocabulary he gives charm to his story. His heart is in his work. He feels what he is writing and therefore makes his readers feel. He makes us share the silent pain of Abraham sacrificing his son. He makes our children flush with intense interest over Joseph in Egypt. From him our Bible gets the story of Jacob and Esau, and to this day he makes the lump rise in our throats as we listen to poor Esau's sobbing cry, " Bless me, even me also, O my father ! " Doubtless the credit is not entirely his. Narratives that had come down to him through many generations of story-tellers would in any case have acquired vivid dramatic interest. But his whole collected history is so full of charm, that we cannot help feeling that this man was a literary artist.

The important thing, however, is that he was much more than an artist. He was a holy saint and prophet of God. He had pondered deeply over life's questions and problems in the light of Jehovah's presence. How did sin enter this beautiful world ? How did the world itself come into being ? Why is woman's highest joy associated with pain ? Above all, what is the relation of God to man—that God whom he felt speaking in his soul? And many noble answers came to him from above. His science was only the science of his time. He had to use the national myths and legends to express his great thoughts. His history cannot always be trusted for accurate details—he could not help that with the sources accessible to him. But no devout reader can peruse the fragments of his book which remain to us without feeling that he was a teacher inspired of God.

He gives us our first written version of the Pentateuch story. The full contents of his book we shall never know since it has gone with the rest of the Lost Books of Israel. But much of it has been disinterred from our present Bible. It evidently began with a Creation Story which is inserted in our Bible, beginning in the middle of the verse, Gen. ii. 4, "In the day that the Lord God (Jehovah Elohim) made the earth and the heavens." Notice the title JEHOVAH which is persistently avoided by the other writers in Genesis. They are evidently influenced by the theory of their day resting on the declaration in Exod. vi. 3. "I appeared to Abraham, Isaac and Jacob by the name of God Almighty, but by My name Jehovah was I not known unto them."

Our author does not seem to know this statement. It does not appear at all in his book. In fact he gives a different theory (Gen. iv. 26), "Then began men to call on the name of Jehovah." At any rate he stands alone in using the name Jahve (Jehovah) in pre-Mosaic story. And to this peculiarity he owes the title by which his work is known, "The JAHVIST (or JEHOVIST) document," which is usually indicated in briefer notation by the letter J.

III

The Bible of Northern Israel. The Jahvist is supposed to have written in the South, in Judah, because the names in that locality are more prominent in his work. About fifty years later some northern prophet or group of prophets wrote a similar work for northern Israel (that is if we may judge again by prominent localities). It was probably somewhere in the days (750–800 B.C.) when Amos and Hosea were preaching in the north. We know less of this work than of its predecessor. We have less of it to judge by. The same earnest spiritual purpose runs through it, but it lacks the vivid personal touch which is the charm of J. It looks as if it were the work of a group of prophets rather than of one.

The first piece we have of it is inserted at Gen. xv., so we do not know whether it went back beyond Abraham. Its story runs parallel with the Judah Bible, though evidently it is using different early sources, for there are discrepancies between the narratives, and it uses different names, *e.g.*, Horeb instead of Sinai; Amorites instead of Canaanites; Jacob instead of Israel.

The most marked difference is the use of the title Elohim (not Jehovah) in all the earlier narrative. Therefore scholars have designated this document as the ELOHIST, which is rather stupid of them, for it only keeps this characteristic in its earlier sections, and it is not the only one to do so, as we shall afterwards see. However, ELOHIST it must remain with its abbreviated title as "E."

The general conclusion of scholars is that it did not long remain a separate book. It seems that later editors very soon after combined it with the Jahvist Bible into one complete narrative, which is conveniently designated by the combined letters JE.

IV

The Book of Deuteronomy. The power of the Word of God is a commonplace in religious history, and seldom has it been better exemplified than in the case of these two rolls, those old lost "Bibles before the Bible." About the time probably of King Hezekiah lived a great unknown student of the life and law of Moses. His bibles were apparently the Bible of Judah and the Bible of Israel (J and E) or probably one book combining them both. For afterwards he wrote the results of his study, and it is evident that these form the basis of his work. But he was greater than his teachers and wrote greater things than they.

We can judge of him the more confidently because his book, unlike the others, has been found intact. As we read it we try to reproduce him for ourselves. An enthusiast for righteousness and an enthusiast for Moses. As St. John spent half a century meditating about Jesus before he put his pen to the story of the Fourth Gospel, so we judge of this man as meditating on God's dealings with Moses till the spirit of the old Legislator lived again in him. His book tells the events of the last month of the Desert wanderings. He gathers into it the essence of the teachings of Moses. He saw the deep spiritual import of that teaching. He brought to it perhaps a still deeper power through the influence of the Spirit of God on himself. The result is the noblest section in the Pentateuch.

We do not know for whom he wrote it, or what he did with it when written. We do not know what influence it had on the people of his day, though there is reason later to conjecture that on its first appearance it had made a deep impression. We know nothing about its history. The manuscript disappeared, and the world might never have known anything about it but for the fortunate accident (humanly speaking) that brought it to light perhaps a century later. The story of its recovery is told in 2 Kings xxii. :—

§ 2. It is a day in the eighteenth year of King Josiah, B.C. 621. Jerusalem is stirring with excitement. No one can talk of anything but the news from the Temple. "*They have found the Book of the Law in the house of the Lord!*" The king had sent down Shaphan the scribe to settle about the workmen's accounts for repairs to the Temple. And after settling the accounts the High Priest showed Shaphan a roll of a book which he had found in some of the Temple chambers during the repairs.

So the King summoned a great gathering of the elders of Judah and Jerusalem to meet him in the Temple for the reading of the Roll.

Then comes the picture of the day of the Assembly. The king is standing by the pillar in the Temple reading in the ears of the crowd the words of the sacred Roll. The chief men of the nation are standing around him, amongst them, most probably, young Jeremiah the prophet, the king's great ally in his work of reform. And wonder and dread fall on them all as they hear. They are evidently deeply stirred and solemnized. "And the king stood by the pillar and made a covenant before the Lord to walk after the Lord and to keep his commandments and his testimonies and his statutes with all his heart and all his soul, to confirm the words of the covenant written in the book. And all the people stood to the covenant."

This is the most striking event in the whole History of the Making of the Bible. Here is evidently a Book regarded for some reason as of divine authority, a book which Josiah and the people clearly regard as an ancient Book of the Law, which had been known before and which had been for a long time lost. The whole story forces that impression on us.

§ 3. But what book was it? The idea that it was our Pentateuch in its present complete form is quite out of the question, for, apart from the evidence which we have of the later composition of the Pentateuch, this was evidently a small book. The whole story, told with the vividness of a contemporary, suggests that it did not take long to read it. Shaphan at once read it. Josiah read it for himself, and then read it for the assembly. Evidently it was not the whole Pentateuch, but a single roll with definite precepts and warnings terse and forcible.

We find that the special reform started by the Roll, especially that of the abolition of the "high places," are just those which the Book of Deuteronomy directs. We find that the writer of the book of Kings, who tells the story directly, quotes twice over from this "Law," *i.e.* from the new-found document, and in each case we find his quotation in our book of Deuteronomy. There is no space here for exhibiting the evidence fully. Suffice it to say that all students of the subject are practically agreed that our Book of Deteronomy, or part of it, was the Roll which Hilkiah found, and which stirred the whole of Jerusalem that day to its depths.

As has been seen, we know nothing about its previous history. All sorts of conjectures have been made, including even the unworthy suggestion that Hilkiah and his friends might have written it themselves and palmed it off on the people as an ancient document! The opinion of our best scholars is that it was a sacred book which had been lost or suppressed probably in the wicked reign of Manasseh or Amon—that it was one of the several editions of the Mosaic story written by some great prophet or prophets from material which they had access to, mainly the Judah and Israel Bibles.

We know it as a book written with passionate prophetic earnestness to rouse the godless nation to enthusiasm for Jehovah. Evidently it made a tremendous impression. The king and his chief helpers made it their banner of reform. Jeremiah the prophet went through the land teaching its precepts (Jer. xi. 1–8). His own writings show deep traces of its influence. Hebrew scholars tell us that a comparative study of the style of the two books shows that Jeremiah had "steeped himself" in Deuteronomy. No other book ever before was such a power in Israel. It was the first appearance of what we may well call a "People's Bible." Other collections of laws and history were in the keeping of prophets and priests. But never before was such a book as this a book for the people, published to the people, telling in noblest form the thoughts of their great Lawgiver, preaching and teaching and beseeching the nation to return to the Lord their God.

V

The Book of the Priests.

We have still one more "Lost Bible" to tell of.

Little more than a century after the finding of Deuteronomy, probably in the days of Exekiel and the Exile, first appeared the "Bible of the Priests," from which our Pentateuch gets the main part of its laws. The Priests were the chief depositaries of laws, part of them oral, handed on at the various sanctuaries from generation to generation, much of them probably written, since the priests were familiar with writing. The book is very decided on the theory that the name Jehovah was not known before Moses. It always calls God, ELOHIM, in Genesis. It records the declaration in Exod. vi. 2, "By My name Jehovah was I not known unto them." We owe to it the majestic Creation story in Gen. i. It seems to have touched very slightly the history of the Patriarchs. It gives special prominence to worship and ceremonial, telling minutely of Circumcision, the Sabbath, the Priesthood and the Festivals. It has a very large collection of laws, mainly ceremonial. The concluding parts of Exodus, the beginning of Numbers, and practically the whole of Leviticus come from it. It is a very systematic work, very particular about chronology and genealogies; and it is a book with splendid lofty ideals. But it looks as if it would be a dull book to read by itself as compared with the stirring pages of Deuteronomy and the Jahvist.

From what we have said of that part of its contents which has come down to us, it will be evident why scholars have designated it the " Book of the Priests," indicated in brief notation by the letter P.

CHAPTER IV

THE RECOVERY OF THE LOST "BIBLES"

HERE it will naturally be asked, If these elementary "bibles" have vanished with the other "lost literature," how can we know anything about them?

The answer is that it is possible in a large measure to reconstruct them by examination of our present Bible, in which they are incorporated. For ancient Semitic historians did not use their material as modern historians do. The modern historian studies all his authorities, digests the material in his mind, and then writes his history in his own words and style, so that we could seldom discover from his book what materials he used. But the ancient Semitic writers pieced together their sources, extracting from each such sections as suited their purpose, lifting them bodily word for word into their work and connecting them where necessary by notes of their own. So that if the documents thus incorporated have any marked characteristics of subject or language or style, it may be possible to distinguish them from one another, and sometimes to reconstruct the original sources word for word.

§ 2. In the next chapter I shall give a New Testament illustration. Here I want to show an Old Testament writer at work. He is writing the Second Book of Chronicles, and has around him, as he repeatedly tells us, the old lost books of Gad and Iddo, and Shemaiah, etc. But, fortunately for our purpose, he has also a book that we know, the First Book of Kings. With it he is using probably some of the others, perhaps only one, which seems likely from some of its references to be the lost Book of Shemaiah. Now watch how he uses them—

THE RECOVERY OF THE LOST "BIBLES"

1 KINGS XIV. 25-28.	2 CHRON. XII. 2-11.
AND IT CAME TO PASS IN THE FIFTH YEAR OF KING REHOBOAM, THAT SHISHAK KING OF EGYPT CAME UP AGAINST JERUSALEM.	AND IT CAME TO PASS IN THE FIFTH YEAR OF KING REHOBOAM THAT SHISHAK, KING OF EGYPT CAME UP AGAINST JERUSALEM *because they had trespassed against Jehovah, with twelve hundred chariots and threescore thousand horsemen, and the people were without number that came with him from Egypt; the Lubiim the Sukiim and the Ethiopians. And he took the fenced cities of Judah and came to Jerusalem. Now Shemaiah the prophet came to Rehoboam and to the princes of Judah . . . and said unto them Thus saith Jehovah Ye have forsaken me therefore . . . Then the princes of Israel and the King humbled themselves . . . And the word of the Lord came to Shemaiah saying, They have humbled themselves, I will not destroy them but will grant them some deliverance and my wrath shall not be poured out on Jerusalem by the hand of Shishak. Nevertheless they shall be his servants that they may know my service and the service of the kingdoms of the countries.* SO SHISHAK KING OF EGYPT CAME UP AGAINST JERUSALEM AND TOOK AWAY THE TREASURE OF THE HOUSE OF JEHOVAH AND THE TREASURES OF THE KING'S HOUSE, HE TOOK ALL AWAY; HE TOOK AWAY ALSO THE SHIELDS OF GOLD WHICH SOLOMON HAD MADE. AND KING REHOBOAM MADE IN THEIR STEAD SHIELDS OF BRASS, AND COMMITTED THEM TO THE HANDS OF THE CAPTAIN OF THE GUARD THAT KEPT THE DOOR OF THE KING'S HOUSE. AND IT WAS SO THAT AS OFT AS THE KING WENT INTO THE HOUSE OF JEHOVAH THE GUARD CAME AND BARE THEM AND BROUGHT THEM BACK INTO THE GUARD CHAMBER.
AND HE TOOK AWAY THE TREASURES OF THE HOUSE OF JEHOVAH AND THE TREASURES OF THE KING'S HOUSE HE TOOK ALL AWAY AND HE TOOK AWAY ALL THE SHIELDS OF GOLD WHICH SOLOMON HAD MADE. AND KING REHOBOAM MADE IN THEIR STEAD SHIELDS OF BRASS AND COMMITTED THEM TO THE HANDS OF THE CAPTAIN OF THE GUARD WHICH KEPT THE DOOR OF THE KING'S HOUSE. AND IT WAS SO THAT AS OFT AS THE KING WENT INTO THE HOUSE OF THE LORD THE GUARD BARE THEM AND BROUGHT THEM BACK INTO THE GUARD CHAMBER.	

§ 3. Here we have a clear illustration of the way in which this Bible historian worked. And because we have one of his documents still existing, it is easy to distinguish between the sources used. But in other parts of the Bible it is not so easy, because all the incorporated documents are lost. Nevertheless it is quite possible, through differences of style, through characteristic words and phrases, and in other ways, not only to distinguish between several sources used, but often even to reconstruct them.

Take the Pentateuch. Begin at the beginning. In the first section, chap. i. to ii. 4, we have a version of the story of Creation in dignified solemn formal style with characteristic words and phrases which also occur in later parts of the book. Amongst them we notice especially the title of the Deity ELOHIM (God).

Now the very next section, beginning Gen. ii. 4, is another Creation story, apparently from a different source. The order of Creation is different, the style is very different, and we are especially struck by the sudden change of the Divine name to JEHOVAH ELOHIM (Lord God).

This at least suggests to us that the Book of Genesis was written, like the Books of Chronicles, by combining earlier sources. Then, as we go on, we find counterparts of these two sections running on still together, keeping still their marked characteristics. We also find repeatedly as in the Creation stories, the same fact doubly recorded and the duplicates apparently belong to these separate counterparts. Here is a good example. Notice the Divine name in each—

GEN. VI. 11–13.	GEN. VI. 5–7.
And the earth was corrupt before **GOD** and the earth was filled with violence. And **GOD** saw the earth and behold it was corrupt for all flesh had corrupted its way upon the earth. And **GOD** said unto Noah The end of all flesh is come before me; for the earth is filled with violence through them and behold I will destroy them with the earth.	And **JEHOVAH** saw that the wickedness of man was great in the earth and that every imagination of the thoughts of his heart was only evil continually. And it repented **JEHOVAH** that he had made man and it pained him at his heart. And **JEHOVAH** said I will blot out man whom I have created.

Sometimes, too, there are discrepancies between these duplicate accounts, *e.g.* in the Creation story, where the order of creation is different—or in the Deluge story, where in one section (vi. 18–22) *one* pair of each kind of animal is preserved, and in another (vii. 1–5) *seven* pair of clean and *one* of unclean. Again in one duplicate the flood covers the earth for twelve months and ten days, and in the other for only sixty-one days. These duplicate sections in their way of putting things, and in their characteristic words and phrases, correspond to the two Creation sections in Gen. i. and Gen. ii. The fact that discrepancies sometimes exist indicates that the respective original authors of these separate accounts did not use quite the same sources of information. At any rate it is quite evident that we have in Genesis at least two earlier accounts used in the same way as these in the Book of Chronicles.

§ 4. Now we are to try to reproduce the lost sources. In an appendix to this chapter will be found a list of the sections allotted by the decision of scholars to one of the separate sources, that one which contains the first chapter of Genesis. Now let us take the first section, Gen. i., and all its corresponding sections through Genesis, as given in this appendix, and with a camel-hair brush tint them all over in a pale red. Then read them consecutively for several pages. We shall find them forming a fairly intelligible story, though very slight and scrappy in the Genesis portion. We shall find characteristic words and phrases running through them, such as: *create, after their kind, the selfsame day, these are the generations of, living creatures, beasts of the earth, creeping thing, all flesh, sojourner, throughout their generations,* etc. There is not very much from this source in Genesis, but if we continue our red sections right through the Pentateuch we shall find in them nearly all the regulations about ritual and ceremonies, about Circumcision and the Sabbath and the Festivals, also the great bulk of the priestly laws. And I trust it will be with some interest we shall feel the conviction that all the old "lost literature" is not altogether lost, that in these red-tinted pages, right through the Pentateuch we have got back at least a large part of the Bible of the Priests.

§ 5. Then we turn back to the Bible to read the parts left uncoloured which also make a fairly intelligible separate story. We cannot doubt that we are reading quite another document, utterly differing from the first in language and style, much more interestingly written, more artistic, more poetical, full of vivid dramatic touches that make the history live before us. We have got back part of the old Jahvist Bible of Southern Judah. Or, rather, perhaps the combination of it with the Elohist Bible of the North.

This little sketch is merely intended to suggest the methods of critical work on the Bible.

APPENDIX TO CHAPTER IV

In Dr. Driver's *Genesis* these are the parts allotted to P—the " Book of the Priests "—

Chap. i. 1–ii. 4ª (creation of heaven and earth, and God's subsequent rest upon the Sabbath) ; v. 1–28, 30–32 (the line of Adam's descendants through Seth to Noah) ; vi. 9–22, vii. 6, 11, 13–16ª, 17ª, 18–21, 24, viii. 1–2ª, 3ᵇ–5, 13ª, 14–19, ix. 1–17, 28–29 (the story of the Flood) ; x. 1–7, 20, 22–23, 31–32 (list of nations descended from Japhet, Ham, and Shem) ; xi. 10–26 (line of Shem's descendants to Terah) ; xi. 27, 31–32 (Abraham's family) ; xii. 4ᵇ–5, xiii. 6, 11ᵇ–12ª (his migration into Canaan and separation from Lot) ; xvi. 1ª, 3, 15–16 (birth of Ishmael) ; xvii. (institution of circumcision) ; xix. 29 (destruction of the cities of the Kik Kār) ; xxi. 1ᵇ, 2ᵇ–5 (birth of Isaac) ; xxiii. (purchase of the family burial-place in Machpelah) ; xxv. 7–11ª (death and burial of Abraham) ; xxv. 12–17 (list of 12 tribes descended from Ishmael) ; xxv. 19–20, 26ᵇ (Isaac's marriage with Rebekah) ; xxvi. 34–35 (Esau's Hittite wives) ; xxvii. 46–xxviii. 9 (Jacob's journey to Padan-aram) ; xxix. 24, 28ᵇ, 29, xxx. 22ª (perhaps) xxxi. 18ᵇ, xxxiii. 18ª (Jacob's marriage with Rachel, and return to Canaan) ; xxxiv. 1–2ª, 4, 6, 8–10, 13–18, 20–24, 25 (partly), 27–29 (refusal of his sons to sanction intermarriage with the Shechemites) ; xxxv. 9–13, 15 (change of name to Israel at Bethel) ; xxxv. 22ᵇ,–29 (death and burial of Isaac) ; xxxvi. in the main (Esau's migration into Edom ; the tribes and tribal chiefs of Edom and Seir) ; xxxvii. 1–2ª, xli. 46 (Joseph's elevation in Eygpt) ; xlvi. 6–27, xlvii. 5–6 , 7–11, 27ᵇ, 28 (migration of Jacob and his family to Egypt and their settlement in the land of Rameses) ; xlviii. 3–6, 7 (Jacob's adoption of Ephraim and Manasseh) ; xlix. 1ª, 28ᵇ–33 ; l. 12–13 (Jacob's final instructions to his sons and his burial by them in the cave of Machpelah).

CHAPTER V

THE CANON OF THE OLD TESTAMENT

I

In the Days of the Exile. WE come now to the final stage in the growth of the Old Testament. I have repeatedly pointed out that two stages must be clearly recognized in the Making of the Bible.

1st. The gradual agelong formation of a religious literature.

2nd. The selection or acceptance or recognition of certain parts of this literature as Divine and authoritative, an inspired Canon or Rule of life and doctrine.

Up to this we have been briefly sketching the first stage. We now come to the second. And here it will be convenient to run over again lightly the line of thought on which we are travelling.

(1) Behind the Bible was a religious community called by God for His great purposes to humanity,

and in which, as in a cherishing home or nest, the Bible was to grow.

(2) In this community, in the Providence of God, arose a primitive literature mainly with a religious purpose, songs and legends and laws and histories, etc.

(3) Later came written collections and selections of this old literature, to what extent we know not —such as the Book of Jasher and the Book of the Wars of Jehovah, etc.

(4) Still later, as the need arose, came fuller books, the Four " Bibles before the Bible,"—like the Four Gospels in the New Testament, committing to writing, just as the Gospels did, a selection of the oral and fragmentary written records of the past.

(5) Beside these was much other literature, in which, most important of all, were the inspired utterances of the Prophets.

(6) THERE WAS NO BIBLE YET, in our solemn sense of the word, only religious literature of varying spiritual value in which some parts stood out more prominently in the estimation of the faithful.

(7) The reason of this prominence was the silent conviction that God was more behind these parts, that they revealed the nature and will of God in an especial manner and degree.

(8) This conviction came not through any

external authority, through any miraculous attestation or any formal decision, but through the persistent appeal of the books or utterances themselves to the Spirit-guided conscience of the community in which they grew. Slowly, gradually, unconsciously that community was making a selection. By the quiet influence of the Holy Spirit on their minds they were preparing for the Making of the Bible.

§ 2. In the day then, when the nation fell and the last of the kings of Judah went away into Captivity, there was still no " Bible." The Jewish Bible, as we have it, belongs to a later day.

Which starts some questionings. How did the Jewish nation live its life without a Bible? I think the reply is that they had their teaching church, their religious services, especially their great Festivals, reminding them of God's dealings in the past. They had the teaching of their priests and, far above all, they had the living voices of the Prophets, the holy men of old who spake as they were moved by the Holy Ghost, declaring to them the Word of God and the presence of God. They did not need a Book religion. The records of the past existed in various fragmentary forms, but the people certainly had no Bible. They did not need it yet. They could not read it even if they had it.

Remember that the English people had no Bible for one thousand years until Tyndale's day. They were taught the Creed and the Gospel story and learned the words of the Psalms. They had their church services and the great ceremony of the Holy Communion, keeping them always in touch with their Lord. The clergy had the sacred books of Scripture from which to teach them. The teaching Church kept religion alive without a People's Bible.

Something like that was the religious life of early Israel. The need of a Bible was not felt. It was not until the prophet voices ceased and the national life was passing away that it was necessary to put down in complete form the great Deeds and Words of the past.

§ 3. Then came the final stage in the Making of the Old Testament. God took that poor faulty Church and nation into Captivity, "apart from the multitude," and prepared them to give to the world their BIBLE. Very wonderful is the working of His Divine Providence. That terrible trouble seems to have done more for Israel than all the years of prosperity. Without it they had hardly been fitted for the Making of the Bible. Their misery brought them closer to God. " The nation as it were went into retreat and performed penance for its long errors and sins." Henceforth idolatry had no power over them. Henceforth the Divine Presence grew more and more real. Henceforth their sacred records grew exceedingly precious as they felt the prophetic voices passing away. There seemed little of national glory to hope for in the future, and so they learned to brood in that sorrowful exile over their wondrous past, to treasure and love as never before the words and deeds of their great leaders of old. They were apart with God and with their Sacred Records. Every word of their prophets, every page of their history was prized. Their deepening spiritual perception made them realize that " unto them were committed the Oracles of God " (Rom. iii. 2). Now they were ready for the final stage, the formation of the Canon of Scripture.

§ 4. The whole environment of our history is now changed. We are no longer in Palestine, the land of Jehovah's worship, the land of Abraham and

Moses and David and the Prophets where the Bible had been growing for a thousand years.

The scene is transferred to gorgeous Babylon, with its pride and pomp and barbaric splendour, with its majestic temples and countless idols and pagan wickedness, where the name of the spiritual Jehovah was not known. There dwelt the exiles in the Jewish quarter by the river.

> "By the waters of Babylon they sat down and wept:
> Yea, they wept when they remembered Zion."

But they did something more than weep about the past. A compelling impulse was upon them from above as they thought of the holy teaching which they had too lightly prized. The prophets were gone, but they would record the sacred words of the prophets. Their history seemed closed, but they would write it for their descendants. Their temple was in ruins, but the priests who preserved the laws and the ritual of its worship would formulate all connected with the service of Jehovah. The loving-kindness of the Lord must never be forgotten; the hope of the mysterious Messiah must still be kept alive.

So they began the writing of the Old Testament. And scarce was their task finished when the Messiah came, in whom lay its chief interpretation and fulfilment. And—it is the bitter irony of history—

when He came they knew Him not—they crucified Him.

§ 5. This collection of Sacred Books was not made all at once, but in three separate periods. The FIRST JEWISH BIBLE was the "Torah," the "Law," our Pentateuch. Later on the chief of the Prophetic Utterances and Prophetic Histories were added. So the SECOND JEWISH BIBLE was "The Law and the Prophets." Later on again it was still further enlarged, and the COMPLETE JEWISH BIBLE was "The Law and the Prophets and the Writings."

In the New Testament titles of the Jewish Bible we see the traces of this gradual formation, *e.g.*, THE LAW (Matt. v. 18; xii. 5, etc.), THE LAW AND THE PROPHETS, or MOSES AND THE PROPHETS (Matt. vii. 12; Luke xvi. 29, 31), THE LAW AND THE PROPHETS AND THE PSALMS (Luke xxiv. 44).

It is also noticeable in the Hebrew Bible where the Books are arranged not as with us, but in the order of their threefold formation—

I. THE LAW (Torah). The five books of Moses.

II. THE PROPHETS (Nebiim).
    (*a*) The Former Prophets, Joshua, Judges, Samuel, Kings.

(b) The Latter Prophets, Isaiah, Jeremiah, Ezekiel and "the Book of the Twelve" (Minor Prophets).

III. THE HOLY WRITINGS (Kethubim).
 (a) The Poetical Books, Psalms, Proverbs, Job.
 (b) The Five Rolls, Canticles, Ruth, Lamentations, Ecclesiastes, Esther.
 (c) The Remaining Books, Daniel, Ezra, Nehemiah, Chronicles.[1]

II

The First Jewish Bible. The first Jewish Bible, then, was quite a small one, only the Pentateuch. With the Jews this has always been *par excellence* "The Bible." No other books have ever won quite the same position in Judaism. The Samaritans have never accepted any other books at all.

We know but little about the process of its formation. We have no history of that wonderful

---

[1] Thus the Books of Chronicles come last of all. It is interesting to see how this explains our Lord's words (Matt. xxiii. 35), the blood of all the prophets shall be required "from the blood of Abel (in the first book of Scripture) to the blood of Zacharias the son of Barachias" (in Chronicles the last book), as though we should say "from Genesis to Revelation."

time of literary activity in the days of the Exile. So we are left to form our conclusions from such hints as we have and from study of the structure of the books as has been touched on in the previous chapters.

Notice first that it was nothing new to them, this idea of inspired Scriptures. I have emphasized the fact that in their earlier history there was as yet no " Bible " in our solemn sense of the word. That is true. And yet, when thus expressed, it is rather an overstatement. For, as we have already seen, the idea of inspired Scriptures—of a Divine authoritative Word of God had in some degree always been with them. There is no doubt that the Ten Commandments stood apart from the beginning as the Divine foundation of the moral law. We are told (1 Kings viii. 9) that in Solomon's time the Tables of stone were still preserved in the Holy of Holies. That very ancient law code, the Book of the Covenant (Exod. xx. 20 to xxiii. 33) was venerated from early times as the Word of the Lord,[1] and the so-called Law of Holiness (Lev. xvii. to xxvi.) in its shorter earlier form probably stood out prominently in the records of the priests. We know

---

[1] This is related by either the Jahvist or Elohist Bible, probably the former. Therefore, in that writer's day, ninth century B.C., it was a story of still earlier days—how much earlier we do not know. See Sanday, *Inspiration*, p. 234.

the words of the prophets were regarded as the Word of Jehovah. And we believe that the fragmentary histories written by early prophets were prized because it was felt that there was something of God in them. But the nearest approach to what we may call written Canonical Scriptures is the great book of Deuteronomy. From the day that it was unearthed in the reign of Josiah it appealed to the deepest spiritual instincts of the nation. For some reason it stood apart as a Divine authoritative Book, in a way that no book had ever done before. We may well regard it as the beginning of the Canon of Scripture. So it will be seen that the thought of an inspired " Bible " was nothing new to the Exiles. But now it was looming larger in their vision. The idea which had taken root in the far past was growing.

§ 2. They had piles of precious manuscripts brought with them into their exile. And prominent amongst their books were the Four Sacred Histories.

The Jahvist book of Judah.

The Elohist book of Israel.

The Book of the Law, which we call Deuteronomy.

The Book of the Priests, written or perhaps completed in the early exile days.

With these Four Books they began. They made from them one great Book which we call the Pentateuch. Why? And how?

Be it remembered that Deuteronomy was already regarded as a sort of national Bible. But it was clearly a very imperfect Bible as it stood. It looked back to laws which it did not quote, and to history which it did not relate. Clearly it was necessary to add these. So, as the other three books were the standard collection of these laws and history, they must in some way be appended. But since they were largely parallel collections, each of them containing much of the same material, it would naturally occur to the writers to make selections and weave them together to avoid repetition.

§ 3. These Four Books suggest irresistibly to us the thought of the Four Gospels in the New Testament. Deuteronomy is very like the Gospel of St. John, a meditative and interpretative work, the other three are parallel histories, like the three Synoptic Gospels. And we can the better understand and put ourselves in the place of the exiles in their literary task if we, with their Four Books, look at a literary work done for the Four Gospels six hundred years later.

Early in the second century A.D., a very famous book was written by a Syrian scholar named Tatian for the convenience of reading in church. It was known as the Diatessaron or Book of the Four. It wove together cleverly the very words of the four Gospels so as to avoid repetition and give a clear consecutive life of our Lord. Here is a section of it—

THEN COMETH JESUS FROM GALILEE TO THE JORDAN UNTO JOHN TO BE BAPTIZED OF HIM.	Matt. iii. 13.
AND JESUS WAS ABOUT THIRTY YEARS OF AGE AND WAS SUPPOSED TO BE THE SON OF JOSEPH.	Luke iii. 23, 24ª
NOW JOHN SAW JESUS COMING UNTO HIM AND SAITH, THIS IS THE LAMB OF GOD WHICH TAKETH AWAY THE SIN OF THE WORLD. THIS IS HE OF WHOM I SAID, AFTER ME SHALL COME A MAN WHICH IS PREFERRED BEFORE ME FOR HE WAS BEFORE ME, AND I KNEW HIM NOT, BUT THAT HE MAY BE MADE MANIFEST TO ISRAEL THEREFORE CAME I BAPTIZING WITH WATER. NOW	John i. 29–31.
JOHN WAS FORBIDDING HIM, SAYING, I HAVE NEED TO BE BAPTIZED OF THEE AND COMEST THOU TO BE? JESUS ANSWERED HIM, SUFFER IT NOW THUS IT BECOMETH US TO FULFIL ALL RIGHTEOUSNESS. THEN HE SUFFERED HIM.	Matt. iii. 14, 15
AND WHEN ALL THE PEOPLE WERE BAPTIZED	Luke iii. 21ª.
JESUS ALSO WAS BAPTIZED, AND HE WENT UP STRAIGHTWAY OUT OF THE WATER AND	Matt. iii. 6.
THE HEAVEN WAS OPENED UNTO HIM. AND	Luke iii. 23ᵇ.
THE HOLY SPIRIT DESCENDED UPON HIM IN THE FORM OF A DOVE'S BODY, AND LO A VOICE FROM HEAVEN, THIS IS MY BELOVED SON IN WHOM I	Matt. iii. 17.
AM WELL PLEASED. AND JOHN BARE WITNESS SAYING, FURTHERMORE I SAW THE SPIRIT DESCENDING AS A DOVE OUT OF HEAVEN, AND IT ABODE ON HIM."	John i. 32.

This was evidently a very convenient book, especially when the Gospels were four cumbrous rolls which had to be hunted over for parallel passages. For a time it was largely used, and in some places almost displaced the separate Gospels. We shall hear of it later. I mention it here to help us to understand how and why the Pentateuch came into being. It is an interesting thought that if the Four Gospels had been lost, like these old Jewish books—and only the Diatessaron remained, we should have exactly the Old Testament problem over again, only in a more difficult form.

§ 4. We believe that God, who was guiding and inspiring His Church for the thousand years before in the growth of the Bible in Palestine, was guiding and inspiring it still in the final work in Babylon. That there was granted to these men an "inspiration of selection." Think of them starting off with that majestic section from the Book of the Priests, " In the beginning God created the heavens and the earth." Think of them solemnly recording ancient narratives which must have seemed childish to their more advanced thought—those simple little stories of the infancy of the human spirit, telling how God walked about in the Garden of Eden, how He talked like a man with Adam and Cain and Noah; how He Himself closed the door of the ark; how He repented Himself and grieved that He had made man, etc. And yet how much poorer the Bible would be without these touching notes of the child races of old and their thoughts about God in His slow progressive revelation of Himself to man!

Year after year their solemn work went on, perhaps in the intervals from Babylonian tasks; around them the noises of the great proud city, in their hearts the peace of prayer and consecration to God. How little could the mighty ones of Babylon think—the " satraps and governors and judges and treasurers and all the rulers of provinces "—that there in that despised Jewish quarter was being done what should be famous when great Babylon was a forgotten name!

If I were going into details I might show that they made the Priests' Book the basis and framework of their new volume and the probability that the Jahvist and Elohist Bibles already brought together had been connected in some form with Deuteronomy before the Exile. But in this simple story such discussions seem unnecessary. Suffice it to say that to their central sacred book of Deuteronomy they appended their Bible compiled from the other three sources, and the result was this book of the Pentateuch which is in our hands to-day.

§ 5. Now see the first appearance in history of this first Jewish Bible.

There is little doubt [1] that this completed Pentateuch was the Book referred to when Ezra went up from Babylon to Jerusalem. "He was a ready scribe in the Law of Moses, the scribe of the commandments of the Lord and of His statutes to Israel, and the Law of his God was in his hand" (Ezra vii.). And again in that thrilling scene at the Feast of Tabernacles (Neh. viii.) when "all the people gathered themselves together as one man to the Broad Place before the Watergate, and they spake to Ezra the Scribe to bring the Book of the Law of Moses which God had commanded Israel." And Ezra, mounting the "pulpit of wood," opened the Book in the sight of all the people, and when he opened it all the people stood up and Ezra blessed the Lord the Great God, and all the people answered Amen, Amen, with the lifting up of their hands, and they bowed their heads and worshipped the Lord. And there was great gladness, and they

---

[1] Though some critics think that Ezra's book was the Priests' Bible, and that the complete incorporation was a little later. But the general belief is as stated above.

kept the feast seven days, and day by day from the first day unto the last he read in the Book of the Law of God."

Here then (457 B.C.) we have the first public appearance in history of our present completed Pentateuch.

§ 6. The reader is, I hope, now in a position to see that this Pentateuch of the Exile days is but a "latest edition," a completest and fullest edition, putting together in literary form earlier existing sacred histories. It is necessary to emphasize this. For in all the disquiet caused by "higher criticism" of the Old Testament, nothing has so disturbed simple Christian people as the statement that the Pentateuch was not written until the days of the Exile.

It is quite true, in a certain sense. But why should it be so disturbing? Take an illustration from secular history. Green's "History of the English People" tells the story of Alfred and of William the Conqueror nearly 1000 years after date. Do we therefore doubt the substantial truth of these stories? Of course we assume that Professor Green used all the earlier English histories, that he and his predecessors used also all accessible older material, ballads and folklore and traditions and laws and letters and ancient charters which bore upon their work.

The Pentateuch comes to us in a somewhat similar way. The writers in that divinely guided community used earlier authorities, and these again used still earlier material back as far as they could go. Behind our Pentateuch, as we have seen, lies an earlier one (JE) belonging to about the seventh century B.C. This has been compiled from two still earlier independent " Pentateuchs " (if I may use the word), J and E, one of them going back to about 900 B.C. These two, again, distinctly state that they used still earlier and evidently independent sources as already pointed out (p. 71). The sources they mention are some of them written documents which even in their day were so ancient as to be ascribed to Moses himself. Other sources were oral traditions or written collections of oral traditions. There is no desire here to minimize the risk of long oral transmission. I have already pointed out that we must make full allowance for this. But it is quite a different thing to doubt that the history is in substance historical, or to suggest that the writers, instead of keeping to the traditions which they had received, were simply inventing ideal pictures for themselves.

This we can say, judging the Bible as we judge

ordinary secular history. But Christian men will also keep in mind that the Bible grew in a community solemnized by the sense of God's presence, and devoutly remembering and recording, however imperfectly, the things that God had done. They will reverently bring in the thought of inspiration and of Divine oversight, and of the connection of the Old Testament with the coming of Christ. And they will remember how our dear Lord Himself loved and reverenced that old Book. Though these things do not guarantee inerrancy in its history, they at least generate an attitude of mind averse to gratuitous suggestions of doubt.

CHAPTER VI

THE COMPLETED JEWISH BIBLE

I

Growth of the Canon. WE have seen the first appearance in history of the completed Pentateuch and watched a great Jew, Ezra, from his pulpit of wood reading this First Jewish Bible. For centuries it was the only Jewish Bible, and to the first generations of its readers seemed likely to remain so. But God had decreed better things.

Now two hundred years have elapsed and we watch another great Jew reading his Bible. But he is finding in it something that Ezra could not find in his. "I understood from THE BOOKS," says Daniel, "the number of the years whereof the Word of the Lord came to Jeremiah" (Dan. ix. 2). Evidently Daniel had in his Bible the prophecies of Jeremiah.

This brings us to the second stage in the formation

of the Canon of Scripture—the Canon of the Prophets.

§ 2. Beside and outside their first national Bible "THE LAW" were the sermons and writings of the prophets. Not only their sermons and prophecies, but the national histories written in the prophet spirit interpreting the relation of Jehovah to the world.

The Prophets, it must be remembered, were not mere *fore*tellers. They were mainly *forth*tellers, preachers of righteousness. And they were not mere enthusiasts. They were in the main practical men, statesmen and patriots who arose in the great crises of the national life to keep men true to the Highest. Above all things they were Seers—men of Divine intuition—as the Bible puts it, men inspired of God. They saw the facts as they were, but they could look beneath the surface and see also what was essential and significant in these facts. By the influence of the Divine Spirit they saw the eternal principles which must for ever guide the life of nations and men, and fearlessly they proclaimed them to their own to all succeeding ages. The truths and principles which they apprehended were so obvious and convincing that each true prophet was absolutely certain of their divine origin. They felt their individuality merged into the Divine personality, and when they spoke they felt it was God speaking through them. That is the meaning of their daring expression "Thus saith the Lord," "Hear ye therefore the Word of the Lord." We too, believe in the truth of their conviction. As the Christian creed puts it, "We believe in the Holy Ghost who spake by the Prophets."

Looking back now we can see how impossible it was that the Pentateuch should remain the whole Jewish Bible with this miraculous phenomenon of prophecy so prominent in the nation proclaiming so directly the Word of the Lord, stirring so deeply the national life. To us the Prophets stand out even higher than the Law, teaching a nobler and more spiritual religion. At any rate it was clearly inevitable that they should some day come into the Bible.

Gradually this conviction grew in the Jewish Church. When the prophets came the people had often opposed them and killed them for their stern rebuking of sin. But afterwards when God's spirit touched them to remorse, and especially when Prophecy became rarer and threatened to die out, then Israel looked back reverently and with loving regret to the great fearless preachers who, as they confessed, had " testified against them to turn them to God " (Neh. ix. 26).

With the great sermons of the prophets the Jews count also their national histories written in prophetic spirit, interpreting the relation of God to men. They believed them to be written by prophets. Therefore they call them the Former Prophecies. And surely we can see why. For these histories not only relate facts, but interpret them, show God behind them. And who but the Seers see God behind the facts of life?

§ 3. Most of the early prophets' discourses were only oral, and therefore have been entirely lost, having doubtless accomplished their purpose in helping the ordinary religious life of the nation. But in God's good Providence the Great Prophecies were preserved, the central expression of Israel's religion, " the culmination of all religion before the time of Christ." Long before the Exile there were collections of the chief prophetic utterances committed to writing by the prophets themselves or their disciples. (See, *e.g.*, Baruch writing down some of the prophecies of Jeremiah (Jer. xlv. 1). And with the increasing spiritual perception of their value came the strong impulse to preserve them from oblivion, though probably with no intention yet to place them in a " Bible " beside the Sacred Law. After the Captivity these collections were compiled and edited, not always very skilfully, as witness the dislocated condition of the prophecies of Jeremiah and the two great sets of oracles brought together under Isaiah's name. The Minor Prophets stood early in a collection by themselves as " The Book of the Twelve."

The prophetic histories (Joshua, Judges, Samuel, and Kings) were the result of a long series of compiling and editing. From the abundant sources quoted in them we can see that there were many earlier histories behind them. Probably these which we have were, humanly speaking, a "survival of the fittest," being those which best recorded the facts and best interpreted the eternal principles behind the facts.

More and more men felt the preciousness of all this prophet literature, and so came the half-unconscious preparation for the " Canon of the Prophets," and the growing recognition of their right to be added to the Bible.

Probably nearly two centuries after the return from the Exile this collection of the Prophets, so long *practically* recognized, became *officially* recognized, and thus THE FORMER PROPHETS, *i.e.* Joshua,

Judges, Samuel, and Kings and THE LATTER PROPHETS, Isaiah, Jeremiah, Ezekiel, and The Book of the Twelve were placed in the Canon of Holy Scripture. It would be tedious to go into details of the history of this period. In any case that history is very obscure. Suffice it to say that somewhere in the third century B.C. is to be placed the official recognition of the Canon of the Prophets as part of the Holy Scriptures inspired by God.

Thus, perhaps 250 years before Christ, came the enlarged Jewish Bible, the "Law and the Prophets," the book in which Daniel found the prophecy of Jeremiah.

II

Completion of the Hebrew Bible.

Now comes the final stage. We have watched the Jew, Ezra, reading the first Bible—"THE LAW." We have watched another Jew, Daniel, two hundred years afterwards, reading the second Bible, THE LAW AND THE PROPHETS. And now, about fifty years after him, we watch a third Jew, away in Alexandria, in Egypt. He is writing (132 B.C.) a translation of an apocryphal book by his grandfather, "The Wisdom of Jesus the son of Sirach," of which we shall hear more later on, and in his preface he mentions three times the Sacred Scriptures of his nation. But notice what he calls them, " The Law and the Prophets *and the others who followed after them,*" and again, " The Law and the Prophets *and the other Books of our Fathers,*" and yet again, " The Law and the Prophets *and the rest of the Books.*"

Evidently the Jewish Bible has again grown or at least is growing. Other books are coming into the Canon of Scripture. And it would appear that the process has been going on for some time, for the writer here assumes that even the Egyptian Jews know of it.

This is our first clear intimation of the third stage in the Making of the Old Testament. Like the other stages it was slow and gradual. It runs on to the beginning of the Christian era.

§ 2. Surely the overruling Providence of God was at the making of that Jewish Bible. In their exaggerated reverence for its first part The Law, one wonders how they ever let any other books in. When the Prophets had got into the sacred enclosure, doubtless they thought their Bible must now be complete. But the God of the Wilderness journey was guiding them still " speaking to the children of Israel that they go forward."

Outside the limits of the Sacred Canon of The Law and the Prophets," there remained an abundant religious literature which could not well come under either of those headings, and which contained phases of spiritual truth not yet included in the Bible. In this literature certain parts had stood out prominent for generations in the reverence and regard of the spiritual in Israel. Doubtless most popular of all was the Psalter. From the older days, from the choir desks of the first Temple [1] had come sheets of psalms and temple music composed by holy men for the service of Jehovah, and if we may judge from the habits of modern choirboys, not always in very good order or preservation. We have a glimpse of the men of Hezekiah in early days picking out from this temple music the psalms of David and Asaph the Seer (2 Chron. xxix. 30). With these were the newer hymns of the second Temple. All these by gradual growth and survival

---

[1] It is sometimes asserted that we have no Psalms before the Exile. But the evidence is very unconvincing. What were the " Songs of Zion " that the exiles refused to sing (Ps. cxxxvii. 3, 4), and the several psalms referring to the king ? See the reference in Isa. lxiv. 11, Jer. xxxiii. 11. See also " the Age of Song and Story " in my earlier chapter. Is it likely that this poetry-loving people had no early psalms ?

of favourites probably grew into the five little hymn-books as indicated in our Revised Version, and it is very likely that they were the first part of this third group of Writings to gain admission into the Canon.

Also amongst this literature were the words of "them that speak in proverbs," writings of ethical and religious interest, the Words of Solomon, the precepts of Lemuel's mother (Prov. xxi. 1), the collection of proverbs made in the great religious movement in Hezekiah's reign (Prov. xxv. 1). There was that wonderful dramatic poem, "Job" grappling with deep questions which men were asking about the mystery of evil. There was the Book of Daniel, which had come too late for admission into "the Prophets," and many other books containing in more or less imperfect form, glimpses of precious spiritual truth. Probably we quite underestimate the amount of such literature and the number of books of collections which were made. There is a suggestive hint in the Book of Ecclesiastes (third century B.C.) "of the making of books there is no end" (Eccl. xii. 12), and we know of a very large number of books of this date which failed to get into the Bible.

§ 3. Of all this religious literature under the overruling Providence of God the best kept rising to the top in the estimation of faithful hearts in Israel. What impulse (humanly speaking) moved them to gather these into their Bible? History does not relate. We can only conjecture; and if we are right, it came again of a great tribulation like the impulse that led them to form their Book of the Law.

Here is a picture from this period of the history. The time is B.C. 168. The trouble is the awful persecution of Antiochus, the mad Syrian king, the raid not chiefly against city or people, but against Jehovah and especially against the holy Manuscripts.

It is an awful story, told by Josephus, told in the Apocrypha in the First Book of Maccabees [1]— a story of the Temple walls spattered with blood, of Bibles torn asunder and burned in the fire, of the fierce fight of men, of the wailing of women, of the altar to Jove in the place of Jehovah, of the great sow slaughtered in insult in the Temple itself, and the broth of its filthy flesh sprinkled on the sacred parchments. We can still read the cry wrung from the hearts of the tortured people—

[1] Josephus, Antiquities xii. 5; Diod. Sic. xxxiv. 1; 1 Maccabees iii.

"O God, the heathen are come into Thy inheritance; Thy holy temple have they defiled and made Jerusalem a heap of stones! The dead bodies of Thy servants have they given to be meat unto the fowls of the air, and the flesh of Thy saints unto the beasts of the land! Their blood have they shed like water on every side of Jerusalem; and there was no man to bury them."[1]

This is not the place to enlarge on that story and to tell of the heroic struggle under Judas the Maccabee—one of the noblest chapters in all Israel's history. We are but conjecturing that in that terrible destruction of the Scriptures the patriot Jews were stirred to an intenser zeal for all their sacred literature, and probably realized more than ever before what a precious treasure had been committed to them.

§ 4. At any rate we know that somewhere in this period came the impulse to gather into their Bible certain of those books which still lay outside it—those which were most loved and venerated by the faithful. We are left much to tradition and conjecture. We have a probably true tradition in a spurious letter prefixed to 2 Maccabees, that

[1] Ps. lxxix., most probably written at this period.

Judas the Maccabee " gathered together for us all those writings which had been scattered by reason of the war." We have the statement (2 Maccabees ii. 13) that Nehemiah, founding a collection of books, gathered together " the writings concerning kings and prophets and the things of David and letters of kings about offerings." But this does not help us in the important question, the raising of certain venerated books into the Canon of Holy Scripture.

We do not know any details. We can only state the result, that about 120 years before Christ, the Old Testament was practically completed by the addition of the " Kethubim " or " Writings," consisting, according to the Jewish list, of—

(a) The Poetical Books : Psalms, Proverbs, Job.

(b) The Five Rolls : Canticles, Ruth, Lamentations, Daniel, Esther.

(c) The remaining Books : Ezra, Nehemiah, Chronicles.

Practically completed, we say, for some books such as Esther and Canticles remained long on the disputed borderland (just like certain New Testament Books, as we shall see later). It seemed at one time probable that Esther and Canticles would have been excluded. It seemed also quite possible that Ecclesiasticus and 1 Maccabees might have got in. There is nothing strange about this. It is quite a natural thing that when a religious community is selecting the books which seem to have most of Divine inspiration, the line of demarcation should sometimes be a little doubtful, that some books should lie for many years on the debateable borderland. These disputed borderland books which failed to gain admission are known as the Apocrypha, which is treated of later on

It was not until the Synod of Jamnia, about 90 A.D., that Esther and Canticles were finally accepted and the list of Old Testament Books officially completed.

Thus, shortly before the coming of the Christ was finished that sacred collection of Books of which He Himself says, " These are they which testify of Me." And then, as if conscious that her mission was accomplished and her national history ended, the Jewish Church closed her Canon of Scripture, giving us the complete Old Testament as we have it to-day.

§ 5. After what has been said in the earlier part of this book, surely no reader needs here to be told that these Scribes and Doctors of the Captivity, or afterwards, did not decide what was to be accepted as the Scriptures of God. Yet at risk of tediousness, let me repeat that these Scribes and

Doctors had very little to do with the decision. The mass of Old Testament Books gained canonical authority because for centuries they had by their own inherent power commended themselves to the spiritual discernment of the godly in Israel. They had long established themselves in the hearts of the faithful with an authority which could not be shaken or confirmed by official decision. The men who compiled the Bible simply accepted established facts. They declared not *what was to be Bible* but *what was already Bible*. They recorded not their own judgment, but that of ages before them. Their verdict only asserted, " These are the books which have been for generations accepted amongst us as of divine authority." In the case of the few controverted books, *e.g.* Esther and Canticles, the authority and the theories of certain Scribes, doubtless played a part, but for the mass of the Old Testament Books the Jewish Church was simply recording the verdict of many generations before them.

§ 6. The earliest Jewish evidence shows that we have exactly their collection of Sacred Books. The most precise is that of Josephus, the famous Jewish historian, who was contemporary with some of the Apostles of our Lord. He gives us the

ARCHBISHOP AELFRIC'S ANGLO-SAXON BIBLE, ELEVENTH CENTURY

complete list of the books in his Jewish Bible which exactly coincide with our list. And he says " Though so long a time has now passed no one has dared to add anything to them or alter anything. But all Jews are instinctively led from the moment of their birth to regard them as decrees of God, and to abide by them and, if need be, gladly die for them."

More important still is the fact that this collection of sacred books was not only the authoritative inspired Bible of the Jewish Church, but also the only authoritative inspired Bible of the Christian Church for very many years until it was again enlarged by the gradual inclusion of the New Testament writings. Our Lord and His Apostles recognize it as " the Scriptures," " the Law and the Prophets," " the Oracles of God." They never hint that this collection of sacred books is imperfect or excessive. They quote it as the inspired teaching of God and the authoritative standard to end all controversy. It is Jesus Himself who bids men search these Scriptures and answers an inquirer's question by referring him to this Bible, " What is written in the Law, How readest thou ? "

PART III
THE APOCRYPHA

THE APOCRYPHA

I

The Apocryphal Books. THIS story of the Making of the Bible would be very incomplete without some account of the Apocrypha, *i.e.* the books which stood nearest in esteem to the recognized Scriptures, but were denied a place in the Canon. From what we have already seen of the way in which certain parts of the religious literature of Israel rose in the religious consciousness to recognition as "Bible," it must be evident that wherever the line had been drawn there must always be some borderland books just outside the boundary. Practically these are what is meant by Apocryphal Books, both in the Old Testament and, as we shall see later, in the New Testament also. The word Apocrypha means "hidden," "kept from public use." Men might "hide" books because of their esoteric teaching, too high for the crowd, or because they were not sufficiently valuable for public instruction. Long essays have been written on the gradations of meaning of the word, but it is not necessary to discuss it here, especially as it is not at all an appropriate title for these books, being much more suitable to another part of this Jewish literature which is called Apocalyptic.

In the last chapter (p. 122) we came on a Jew writing a preface to a religious book written by his grandfather, Jesus the son of Sirach. We were not concerned at all there with this book of his grandfather. But we are here. For this book (Ecclesiasticus) was probably amongst the first, and certainly amongst the best, of all the books of the Apocrypha. Here is the list of the books commonly known by that name—

1 AND 2 ESDRAS.	BARUCH.
TOBIT.	SONG OF THE THREE CHILDREN.
JUDITH.	
REMAINDER OF ESTHER.	STORY OF SUSANNA.
THE WISDOM OF SOLOMON.	BEL AND THE DRAGON.
THE WISDOM OF JESUS THE SON OF SIRACH (ECCLESIASTICUS).	PRAYER OF MANASSES.
	1 MACCABEES.
	2 MACCABEES.

Their position varies very much in the different sections of Christendom. In the Roman Church the Apocryphal books stand with the inspired books of the Hebrew Scriptures in equal position and authority; the usage of the Greek Church seems to vacillate between the Roman position and that of their own official Longer Catechism which relegates these books to a subordinate position; the Church of England places them as a sort of appendix to the Old Testament, not as canonical Scriptures, but as books useful for edification; while the various churches of Protestantism reject them altogether. I merely note these positions here. We shall discuss them later on.

§ 2. But whatever position be assigned to them the Apocryphal books ought to be known a good deal better than they are. The fact that they have been a part—though an inferior part—of the Christian Bible from the beginning to this day should be a sufficient reason. But there are other reasons.

These books form a prominent part of the Jewish religious literature in the age just before Christ, and are therefore an important aid towards understanding that age, and " putting ourselves in the place " of the Jews at the impact of Christianity. They carry on the Jewish history and literature over the gap after prophecy ceased, and illustrate the way in which religious ideas kept growing. For instance, the scant teaching about the future life in the Old Testament makes us rather surprised at the Pharisees' profession of belief in the Resurrection and angels and spirits (Acts xxiii. 8). But this literature shows us that the belief had rapidly grown in the interval and was considerably helped by these apocryphal books. The chief New Testament word for Resurrection (ἀνάστασις) appears first in the Second Book of the Maccabees. And it is the Apocrypha which gives us that fine Church lesson read on All Saints' Day—

> "The souls of the righteous are in the hands of God, and there shall no torment touch them. In the sight of the unwise they seemed to die. Their departure is taken for misery and their going from us to be utter destruction, but they are in peace. For though they be punished in the sight of men yet is their hope full of immortality. And having been a little chastised they shall be greatly rewarded, for God proved them and found them worthy of Himself" (Wisdom iii.).

The Apocrypha traces also for us a distinct advance in the ideals and the aspirations after a Messiah, as also does the other religious literature of the same period which is called "Apocalyptic." The Book of Enoch,[1] for example, not only shows a strong Messianic hope and uses the names "the Christ" and "the Just One," but actually gives us the first use in Jewish literature of the title

---

[1] Not in the Apocryphal list, but belonging to the Apocalyptic literature of that period. See Jude ver. 14.

which our Lord loved to appropriate to Himself, "the Son of Man." What a light is thrown on that title and on the tense expectation of a Messiah and on the mysterious spirit of prophecy in the Jewish Church before He came—when one reads in this Book of Enoch (about second century B.C.) !—

> " And there I saw One who had a Head of Days and His head was white like wool, and with Him was another Being whose countenance had the appearance of a man and His face was full of graciousness like one of the holy angels. And I asked the angel who went with me and shewed me all the hidden things, concerning the Son of Man, who He was and whence He was and why He went with the Head of Days. And he answered and said unto me: This is the Son of Man, who hath righteousness, with whom dwelleth righteousness and who reveals all the treasures of that which is hidden, because the Lord of Spirits hath chosen Him and His lot before the Lord of Spirits hath surpassed everything in uprightness for ever. And this Son of Man . . . will arouse the kings and mighty ones from their thrones and will loosen the reins of the strong.
>
> " And at that hour that Son of Man was named in the presence of the Lord of Spirits and His Name was before the Head of Days. And before the sun and the signs were created, before the stars of the heaven were made, His Name was named before the Lord of Spirits. He will be a staff to the righteous in which they will support themselves and not fall, and He will be the light of the Gentiles and the hope of those who are troubled of heart. All who dwell on the earth will fall down and bow the knee before Him, and will bless and laud and celebrate with song the Lord of Spirits. And for this reason had He been chosen and hidden before Him, before the creation of the world and for evermore" (Enoch xlv. 1-5, xlviii. 2, 6. Charles' Translation).

§ 3. The Book of Enoch, though not in the Apocryphal books bound up with our Bibles, is a specimen of the religious literature of which the Apocrypha formed part.

In the best of the Apocryphal books there is much of sound practical religious advice in the little details which compose human life. God and Right and Duty and Self-sacrifice and Discipline are prominent notes in the teaching. If the fashionable literary faddists who write and talk so much of the pagan " Wisdom-books " of the East, would study beside them the Wisdom-books of the Apocrypha, it should considerably profit them.

It is worth while noticing also a certain literary interest connected with the Apocrypha. Such well-known expressions as " A Daniel come to Judgement ! " " He that touches pitch shall be defiled," " Magna est veritas et prævalet," the hymns " Now thank we all our God," " Jesus, the very thought of Thee," originate in these books, while Handel's great composition " See the Conquering Hero comes " is for ever associated with the hero days of the Maccabees.

§ 4. What has been here said must not, however, be taken as generally applying to all these books. They are very unequal in value. While such books as Ecclesiasticus and Wisdom seem fitted to stand side by side with some of the later Old Testament, and I Maccabees is the grandest story in history of a great soldier of God, there are others which are very puerile and silly in spite of sensible religious teaching in them. It is said that there was a time when I Maccabees and Ecclesiasticus seemed likely to find a place in the Jewish Canon of Scripture, and if it were so one does not wonder at it. But it is quite possible to overdo our appreciation of the Apocrypha as a whole. Some of it is very inferior, and, as we read it, we may be thankful that a higher than human wisdom guided the Making of the Bible.

II

The Apocrypha in the Jewish Bible.

Let us glance briefly at its history. It must be clearly understood that the Return from the Exile in the days of Ezra and Nehemiah only meant the return of a comparatively small minority. The bulk of the exiles remained in their new home. Perhaps they were not the most earnest and religious, but it is very likely that they were the wealthiest and ablest business people. They prospered much in Babylon, and generation after generation, with the keen instinct of the Jews, they extended themselves for trading purposes over the chief cities of the East till almost every civilized nation had its share of them. Like the " Greater Britain," which we speak of beyond the seas, so was the " greater Israel " spreading through the civilized world, vastly outnumbering the Palestine stock, but ever looking back to Jerusalem as exiles to their home. We form some idea of their numbers and the extent of their wanderings as we watch a group of them one day who had come back to Jerusalem for Pentecost, " Parthians and Medes and Elamites and dwellers in Mesopotamia, in Judea and Cappadocia, in Pontus and Asia, in Phrygia and Pamphylia, in Egypt and the parts of Libya about Cyrene, strangers from Rome both Jews and Proselytes, Cretes and Arabians." [1]

This " Greater Israel " is what is known in the New Testament as the " Diaspora," or Dispersion, that great outside world of Jews to which the Epistles of James and 1 Peter were addressed-Everywhere they carried with them their religion, and especially their sacred Book of the Law, as we read, " Moses hath in every city them that preach him being read in the synagogues every Sabbath day." [2]

[1] Acts ii. 9. [2] Acts xv. 21.

It is impossible to exaggerate the vast influence of this " People of the Dispersion " in the founding of Christianity. Here was the ground prepared all over the heathen world, the worship of the One God and the prominence of the Holy Scriptures which were the preparation for the Messiah. And, here, too, in one of the cities of the Dispersion young Saul of Tarsus was being prepared for his life work.

§ 2. The two chief centres of this Greater Israel were Babylon and Alexandria, and the latter is the place chiefly connected with the story of the Apocrypha. When Alexander the Great, with statesmanlike foresight, had taken the Egyptian fishing village of Rhacotis and founded there his magnificent port and city, he settled in it large numbers of Jews. These grew rapidly, and were steadily reinforced by emigrants from the homeland, until Alexandria became largely a Jewish city. Fully half the inhabitants were Jews. It was a new "Israel in Egypt" set at the very heart of the Empire.

But as generation after generation passed, the exiles far away from the fatherland lost touch altogether with their national language. Greek was the universal language of the time, therefore they knew Greek the language of their neighbours, and did not know Hebrew except as a classic. And therefore it became necessary, if they were to have a People's Bible, that that Bible should be in Greek. Now the King of Egypt, Ptolemy Philadelphus (B.C. 250), was friendly to the Jews, and took a deep interest in their history and literature. So he got the Hebrew Bible translated into Greek for his great library, and thus began the famous Greek Bible, the LXX or Septuagint, which afterwards played so large a part in Judaism and Christianity.

§ 3. Naturally, in a world so largely Greek speaking, the influence of Greek learning and Greek culture and Greek ideas would be very strong. Even in Palestine, where we should least expect it, it appeared surrounding and in some degree sapping the rigid Hebrew exclusiveness. There were two opposing tendencies; the spirit of strict rigid, almost fanatical Judaism, and the spirit of easy tolerance and " liberal thought," and sympathy with Gentile learning. The Pharisee of our Lord's day is the representative of the one, the Sadducee of the other.

The Greek spirit, with its easy tolerant, liberal attitude, had in it the seeds of great things, good and evil. Its tendency was to make bridges between the strict Hebrew religion and the broadness of Gentile philosophy, "Your heathen sages, too, were taught of God," the liberal Jew would say; "And your great prophets," the Greek would reply, "were, like our sages, seeking after Truth." In the providential preparation for a world-wide religion there was much good in this. It broke up the Jewish exclusiveness, it made possible broader thoughts of God, it prepared for the revolutionary work of St. Paul.

And yet it was a dangerous tendency too. For its easy graceful tolerance had not much depth of spiritual knowledge or conviction behind it. The sense of God, the agonizing sense of sin, the sense of separation from an evil world, all that which the discipline of ages had wrought into the life-blood of Israel meant little or nothing to the polished easy-going Gentiles seeking in their own light way the beautiful and the good. In a man like Saul of Tarsus, his broader training led to blessed results for the Church, but in smaller men there was a risk of obliterating the deepest things that Israel was to teach to the world.

§ 4. It is easy then to understand that the foreign Jews living for centuries in close friendly intercourse with the Gentile people around them would be likely to lose a good deal of strict Jewish exclusiveness. It would be especially likely in Alexandria, which was a great centre of Greek learning. At first it would have no effect at all upon their Bible, for their first Bible was only the sacred Law. They would be as strict about that as their brethren in Palestine. One could not imagine a faithful Jew anywhere allowing the Book of the Law to be tampered with, or any new book to stand near its sacred words.

But the later books were not to them in the same position as the Law. And these later books too were only in the process of coming into the Bible. The boundary line had not yet been drawn. And so one can understand if a new book teaching high thoughts about God and religion should grow into the spiritual affections of the Jews of Alexandria, they would be much less startled than their Palestine brethren at the idea of letting it circulate along with their Scriptures. The Palestine Jews felt that a special Divine inspiration was the essential requisite, and so they closed their canon when prophecy ceased. But the Alexandrian Jew, in his "liberal" surroundings, had laxer views. It was the saying of the famous Jew, Philo of Alexandria, "Every good man is inspired," and it is easy to see how that tendency would be likely to let into the Bible books which they would not look at in Palestine. The LXX Bible was growing. The later part of the Jewish Canon was coming into it, but rather loosely, without any unity of plan. And by degrees there crept in one by one into successive editions the rather good and edifying books which we now call the Apocrypha.

So the Apocrypha got into the Greek "Bible of the Dispersion," but never into the Hebrew Bible. It was accepted in Alexandria, but never in Palestine. There it, and the Bible which contained it, were regarded as "an abomination worse than the worship of the golden calf."

III

The Apocrypha in the Christian Church.
Then came Christianity, and the Old Testament was its Bible. But the vast majority did not know Hebrew. Therefore they had to use the Greek Septuagint. And therefore they grew accustomed to the Apocryphal books bound up with it. And therefore it was almost inevitable that they should accord them a quasi-recognition. If we should bind up Thomas à Kempis for two centuries

with the New Testament, it would require very frequent reminders to keep it in its true position.

Here let us avoid a common misunderstanding. Since we know from their quotations that the apostles used the LXX it is often assumed that they had the Apocrypha in their Bibles. But it has to be remembered that they were strict Jews of Palestine. And we have clear evidence of a Palestine LXX with only the books of the Hebrew Scripture in it.[1] Doubtless they knew some of the Apocryphal books. What patriotic Jew would be ignorant of, *e.g.*, the Story of the Maccabees? But acquaintance with a religious literature is a very different matter from taking it as authoritative inspired Scripture. At any rate, amid all the large mass of quotations in the New Testament from the Old there is not one single direct quotation from any book of the Apocrypha.[2]

§ 2. We glance now very briefly at the position of these books in a few prominent parts of the

[1] *E.g.*, the canon of Melito, A.D. 172, and see Westcott, "Bible in the Church," p. 124.

[2] Jude ver. 14 is no exception, as Enoch is not included in the Apocrypha. Jude is quoting probably words which his readers would be familiar with just as Paul quoted from the Greek poets Aratus and Epimenides (Acts xvii. 8, Titus i. 12).

Church at different times. What we shall mainly find is that the leaders and thinkers in the Church frequently point out the distinction between them and the Canonical Scriptures, but that in popular usage the distinction is very much forgotten and more so as the Jewish element becomes less prominent in the Church.

In later chapters on the New Testament history we shall see, about the year 200 A.D., three great churchmen, Irenæus, and Clement, and Tertullian, in widely separated churches. Let us hear what men of their day thought about the Apocrypha. Irenæus, Bishop of Lyons in Gaul, sometimes assumes that the LXX contains only the Hebrew Canonical books. Yet he quotes three of the Apocrypha with the undoubted Scripture. Clement of Alexandria, the city where the Apocrypha started, of course quotes its books. And the third of them, Tertullian from Northern Africa, has the Apocrypha in the Bible version of his church.

It is worth noticing especially that version of the African Church, the "Old Latin," as it is called, for it had an important bearing on the Apocrypha question two hundred years later. This Old Latin version was made direct from the Alexandrian LXX, and consequently contained the Apocryphal books, and this Church of North Africa, being so isolated from the Eastern Churches, seemed to consider that the LXX was the original Scriptures. As this "Old Latin" version extended widely, even in later days as far as England and Ireland, its influence on the position of the Apocrypha was very considerable. We shall hear of it again later in the days of St. Jerome.

§ 3. Now we move on another hundred years. Eusebius, the famous church historian, is bishop of Cæsarea, about 340 A.D. He is a great student of the Canon of Scripture. In three separate places he gives lists of the Canonical Scriptures, and in every case omits the Apocrypha. He refers to some of its books as "disputed," and yet at another time he is quoting from the book of Wisdom as if it were Scripture.

Cyril, Bishop of Jerusalem, half a century later, is very positive against the use of the Apocrypha as Canonical Scriptures. Probably the question was prominent at the time. "Learn from the Church," he says, "what are the Books of the Old and New Testament, and I pray you read nothing of the Apocryphal books. . . . For the translation of the Divine Scriptures which were spoken by the Holy Spirit was accomplished through the Holy Spirit.

Read the twenty-two books which these rendered, but have nothing to do with Apocryphal writings."

Look back again now after one hundred years at the Church of Alexandria, the home of the Apocrypha, and hear the wise measured words of Athanasius, its great Archbishop, " All the Books of the Old Testament are in number twenty-two " (here he gives the list of the Canonical Books as in our Old Testament to-day, and goes on), " there are also other books not included in these nor admitted into the Canon which have been framed by the fathers for the benefit of those approaching Christianity ; the Wisdom of Solomon—Wisdom of Sirach, etc.

Now we turn to Rome. It is especially important for us Westerns to know the attitude of the Roman Church in the centre of the Western world. Ruffinus, a well-known ecclesiastical writer there, A.D. 410, gives in one of his books the Old Testament list exactly as we have it, and adds, " There are other books called by the ancients, not Canonical, but Ecclesiastical, *i.e.* Wisdom, Tobit, Judith, etc."

But much more important is the pronouncement of the famous Jerome, the greatest scholar and critical student of the Roman or any other Church. Pope Damasus, A.D. 383, set him to work at revising the " Old Latin " Bibles of which we have already heard (p. 149). A few years later he began a more important work, the translation of the Old Testament direct from the original Hebrew, a work of vital import to the whole Western Church. For this was the beginning of the great Vulgate Version, the Bible of Europe for one thousand years. Now note what he says in his preface—it will be important to remember when we come to the Council of Trent. After mentioning the twenty-two books as we have them to-day, he adds, " Whatever is beyond these must be reckoned as Apocrypha. Therefore, the books, Wisdom, Judith, etc. . . . are not in the Canon;" and again, "the Church reads these books for the edification of the people, not for the authoritative confirmation of doctrine." That was surely decisive enough in the leading scholar of the Roman Church.

There was a good deal of feeling on the part of those accustomed to the popular use. But Jerome was a stiff fighter, and his epistles show how sharply he could hit back. Yet in spite of himself he was influenced in some degree by the feeling of his friends, and though at first he had refused to revise any but the Canonical Books, he was prevailed on to make a hurried revision of Tobit and Judith for his great Bible. As the years went on, when the old fighter was long in his grave, the other books were inserted out of the Old Latin Bible. Therefore the *modern* Vulgate, in spite of St. Jerome's opinion, contains the Apocrypha mingled with the other books.

§ 4. We now pass over one thousand years to the Middle Ages and the Reformation. Of the intervening period there is not much to tell. Church leaders here and there emphasized St. Jerome's distinction between the books; but in popular usage it was largely ignored. In the Western Church it is worth noting that the prominent Roman theologian, St. Thomas Aquinas, in the thirteenth century, was one of those who helped to keep the Apocrypha in its secondary place. The Eastern, that is the Greek, Church was rather careless and indefinite, though tending mainly to distinguish between the books. For its present position Bishop Westcott[1] quotes the official Russian Church catechism which separates the Apocrypha after the example of Athanasius as forming a useful preparatory study to the Bible.

But we are mainly concerned with the Roman Church and the famous decision of the Council of Trent (1546), the vital point in the story of the Apocrypha. Europe was convulsed in the throes of the Reformation, and the Council was considering

[1] "Bible in the Church," p. 229.

the whole position. On February 12, 1546, they had before them the Luther's article affirming that only the Hebrew Canon of the Old Testament and the acknowledged Books of the New Testament ought to be admitted as authoritative. This was discussed at four meetings. It was not an easy question. Their best theological scholars, Cardinal Ximenes, in his magnificent Polyglot Bible, and Cardinal Cajetan, the stern opponent of Luther, both held to the position put forth by St. Jerome. But popular feeling was averse to that pronouncement, and some of the popes had given utterances on the other side. Perhaps if Luther had been out of it, things would have been different. But at any rate we have but to record the famous decision of the Council on the 8th of April, 1546. "The holy Ecumenical and General Council of Trent, following the example of the Orthodox fathers, venerates *all* the Books of the Old and New Testament . . . with an *equal* feeling of devotion and reverence." Then comes the list of the Books, including those of the Apocrypha, and the decree closes with an anathema on all who in future shall not receive the entire books as *equally inspired Scripture.* "This fatal decree," says Bishop Westcott, "in which the Council, harassed by the fear of lay critics and grammarians, gave a new aspect to the whole question of the Canon was ratified by fifty-three prelates, amongst whom there was not one German, not one scholar distinguished for historical learning, not one who was fitted by special study of the subject in which the truth could only be determined by the voice of antiquity."

§ 5. With a statement of the Anglican position this sketch of the Apocrypha may close. It is the position stated so definitely by St. Jerome, the position in the main of the great leaders all down the history of the Universal Church. It is stated clearly in the Sixth Article—

> "In the name of Holy Scripture we understand these canonical books of the Old and New Testaments of whose authority was never any doubt in the Church—*Genesis, Exodus*, etc. (as in English Bible), and the other books (as Jerome saith), the Church doth read for example of life and instruction of manners, but yet doth it not apply them to establish any doctrine. Such are the following :—The Third Book of Esdras, The Fourth Book of Edras, The Book of Tobias, etc. (here follows the list of Apocrypha, as we have inserted here (p. 136).
> "All the Books of the New Testament as they are commonly received we do receive and account them canonical."

That is to say, the Apocrypha is sanctioned for Ecclesiastical use, but not as a rule of doctrine. On certain days portions of it are read in the Church lessons, but the Church does not apply it to establish any doctrine.

In all her versions of Holy Scripture from Tyndale down to the Authorized Version, the Apocrypha is printed by itself as an appendix to the Old Testament. The Bible of the whole Catholic Church is not complete without it. At the Coronation of King Edward the Bible Society sent a magnificently bound Bible as a Coronation gift, and it had to be returned as it was without the Apocrypha. This then is the position of the Old Testament Apocrypha in the English Church, and so far as we can learn in the Greek Church, and this has been its position in the whole Christian Church from earliest days, a subordinate position—Ecclesiastical not Canonical—for Edification, not for doctrine.

There is no New Testament Apocrypha in the Bible, which seems rather anomalous. The New Testament had just as good books left outside its Canon and marked Apocrypha, but they have dropped out and been forgotten.

PART IV
THE MAKING OF THE NEW TESTAMENT

CHAPTER I

THE NEW TESTAMENT

WHERE the story of the Old Testament closes, the story of the New Testament begins. They touch at the centre-point in the history of the world when

" IN THE FULNESS OF TIME GOD SENT FORTH HIS SON."

The first thing that strikes one in the Making of the New Testament is that, like that of the Old, it was unconscious, unintentional. When we come to Apostolic days we find the first Christians with their complete Holy Bible which we now call the Old Testament. And to one who really thinks himself into their position, the wonder is, humanly speaking, that there should ever have come what we call the New Testament. For these early Christians had no more notion of making a new Bible or adding to the old one than we have to-day. They had, as we have, the Word of God, believed to be complete, regarded by them and quoted by

Christ and His Apostles as the Bible of Divine authority. They wanted no other. It would have seemed to them sacrilegious to add to it even if they thought of such a thing, which they did not.

The curious thing though is, that they did not want (even without putting it into a Bible) to write at once for their own use a full life of Jesus. One would have expected that the first thing they would do after Pentecost would be to go to the twelve Apostles and ask them, "Write us down in a book at once everything that you have seen and heard and learned about Jesus during those wonderful three years." But they did not. Perhaps it will surprise us less if we try to put ourselves in their place.

1

The Oral Gospel. Take the first twenty years after the Ascension up to about A.D. 50. Here is a religious community scattered in groups through many cities and villages—simple plain people, fishers and farmers and porters and tentmakers and artisans. They are very happy in their wonderful new religion. One thought dominates all life for them. "We know that the Son of

God is come."[1] They want to hear everything they can about Him. Most of them cannot read. Very few would be capable of writing a book. In any case they do not want books. In Palestine, at least, they have a strong prejudice against committing anything to writing. Their whole training has been oral. Their knowledge of things has come by hearsay. There are no newspapers. When there is any news somebody tells it. Written books or read books (except the Bible) are not at all in their line.

Also it is hardly worth while writing books. Mingled with their new joy is a restless expectancy. They are convinced that Jesus will return during their lifetime to take them all to heaven. They do not know the moment. It may be any day, "at evening or at midnight or at cockcrow, or in the morning." Even their Apostles at first looked forward to the day when "we which are alive and remain shall be caught up to meet the Lord in the air."[2] So, with heaven lying about them there was no need of writing books for the future. There was no future, except a future in glory with the Lord.

[1] 1 John v. 20.
[2] 1 Thess. iv. 17.

§ 2. So they came together in their little weekly assemblies to hear their Old Testament Scriptures and to pray and to receive their Holy Communion and to listen to the burning words of the "Witnesses" who had been with Jesus or seen him or learned about Him from those who had. They wanted not written documents, but heart to heart talks from men who knew. Sometimes they had only a teacher who had learned from the Apostles. Sometimes they had a disciple who had actually heard the Lord. And sometimes they would get hold of a real live Apostle, one of the Twelve. That was a great day, when Peter or James or John or Philip was present in the town. Nobody would stay at home that day. Think of John telling how he had stood by the Cross and heard the dying words of the Lord; or Peter telling of that miserable night of his denial when the Lord turned and looked upon him; or Philip picturing the joy and enthusiasm of the first Easter morning.

I suppose that was a good deal what was meant by "preaching Christ," the one great subject of all their preaching. Daily in the Temple and in every house they ceased not to teach and preach Jesus Christ.[1] At Antioch they spoke to the Grecians, "preaching the Lord Jesus;"[2] "they preached Jesus and the

[1] Acts v. 42.   [2] Acts xi. 20.

Resurrection." [1] "We preach not ourselves," says Paul, " but Christ Jesus the Lord." [2] They could not always be sketching the whole scheme of redemption. Much of their teaching must have been the narrating of separate incidents in the Lord's life. As we shall see later, Peter is said to have " framed his teaching to meet the immediate wants, but not making a connected narrative of our Lord's discourses " (p. 177).

Now it is a matter of experience that if any man keeps telling the same incidents for many years there comes naturally a certain uniformity in the telling, almost as fixed as writing. And if the several Apostles were continually teaching the life of Jesus there would gradually come a certain uniformity in the cycle of teaching. They could not dwell on every little point. They would " put first things first." Special acts and discourses of the Lord would stand out in higher prominence. Other incidents of minor importance would fall into the background and be dropped out. The Incarnation, the Baptism, the Passion, the Resurrection, the Ascension, the historic substance of the ancient creeds, would be the great centres around which the teaching grouped itself. Thus, in course of years, there would be a growingly uniform cycle of facts

[1] Acts xvii. 18.   [2] 2 Cor. iv. 5.

and sayings which would be the main Gospel of the Church, stored in the memories of the hearers.

Then again every year in a hundred places together, were the Preparation classes for Baptism. Converts had to be taught in regular and compact form the main facts of the Christian creed. This would greatly tend towards crystallizing the oral teaching into a fairly uniform gospel known well by all instructed Christians all over the Church.

§ 3. Thus came the formation of an ORAL GOSPEL differing somewhat in different places and periods, but in the main the same. This was the "deposit," the matter "which they delivered, which from the beginning were eyewitnesses and ministers of the Word." This was what Paul was orally taught by Ananias at Damascus and by others more fully afterwards. "I delivered unto you," he says to the Corinthians, "that which I also received, how that Christ died for our sins according to the scriptures; and that He was buried, and that He hath been raised on the third day according to the scriptures."[1] This is what he means when he bids the Thessalonians, "Hold fast the traditions which ye have received." This is the deposit about

[1] 1 Cor. xv. 3, 4.

which he charges Timothy, "O Timothy, guard that deposit which is committed unto thee."[1]

This was the ORAL GOSPEL published through the whole Church, not in written books, "but on the fleshly tablets of the heart." Probably our present Gospel of St. Mark would fairly represent its main substance. Mark, as we shall see later, is said to have learned it from the "lessons" or oral instructions of Peter. At any rate this oral deposit was the only gospel the Church had for thirty years. So far as we can judge neither Paul nor Peter, nor perhaps any of the apostles except John, ever saw one of our written gospels. They certainly give no indication of it. If Paul knew of written gospels he would hardly have exhorted the Thessalonians to hold fast the oral traditions, or deliver to the Corinthians only that which he had orally received.

II

The Epistles. Now we come to the next stage— the stage of the first Christian writings, the Epistles—beginning, say, about the year 50 A.D. These were the first written part of the New Testament.

[1] 1 Tim. vi. 20.

The various needs and perplexities of the scattered churches called forth letters of advice and direction and instruction, written mainly for the immediate occasion and in answer to letters of inquiry received. There was no thought of them as Bible or Scripture or Sacred. They were simply letters of the great missionary Apostles to the communities which they had visited and evangelized.

I picture to myself the writing of the first Christian Scripture. It is A.D. 48. A wiry little man with weak eyes is seated in a room working at pieces of black haircloth material for tents. He has his work to do, and perhaps he can think better that way, as a woman can think better with her knitting in her hands. He is dictating a letter while he works. Busy people then, as now, dictated when they could instead of writing, and probably Paul's weak eyes would make it more necessary for him. At any rate we know it was his custom, and it has been suggested that perhaps his vividness and directness of language, his broken constructions and sudden changes of subject, may be in some measure the result of it.[1]

Two young men are with him—Timothy and Silvanus. Silvanus can probably write best, as

---

[1] Milligan, "New Testament Documents," p. 26.

we find indications afterwards that he wrote for Peter.[1] Probably it is he who is writing now for Paul, with a roll of papyrus before him about three feet long made from the pith of papyrus reeds pasted together. Parchment was not used for letters, and in any case would be too dear for poor people. But he could buy papyrus in the shops, as we buy foolscap, from six to eighteen inches wide and of any length required. We can judge the sizes by the papyri that have been discovered.

So Paul is dictating and Silvanus is writing on the papyrus roll in little columns two or three inches wide :—

"PAUL AND SILVANUS AND TIMOTHY UNTO THE CHURCH OF THE THESSALONIANS IN GOD THE FATHER AND THE LORD JESUS CHRIST. GRACE TO YOU AND PEACE."

How little those two men thought that day that they were writing the first words of the great Christian Scriptures for all the world and for all the ages! We do not know that this was the first Church letter that Paul wrote. Some have been lost. But this is the first that we know of.

§ 2. A.D. 54. Again Paul is dictating a letter, a much larger and more formidable one. It is the Epistle to the Romans. This time I do not imagine

---
[1] 1 Peter v. 12.

he had any tentwork in his hands, for he has to concentrate hard. And this time we have not to guess at his secretary's name, for it is signed, " I, Tertius, who write the epistle, salute you in the Lord." [1] We can even make a guess at the messenger who carried it. " I commend to you Phœbe, our sister, a deaconess of the church at Cenchrea : that ye receive her in the Lord, and help her in whatever matter she needs." [2] Apparently Phœbe was travelling to Rome along the great Roman roads or by the vessels of one of the shipping companies navigating the Mediterranean. Who more likely to carry the letter?

Thus the epistle reached Rome, and surely it was eagerly read next Sunday, and probably for several Sundays. Not in the place of Holy Scriptures. Certainly not. That position did not come to it until many years later. But rather as a discourse or sermon written by their great missioner. Probably they would find it a much stiffer sermon than the simple gospel narratives which they were accustomed to hear as sermons. Perhaps it was one of the audience that day who tells us later that " in the epistles of our beloved brother Paul are some things hard to be understood." [3]

---

[1] Ch. xvi. 22.   [2] Ch. xvi. 1.
[3] See 2 Pet. iii. 16, whose author is not certainly known.

And when they had read it repeatedly they would lend it to another church (cf. Col. iv. 16). But it had to be handled carefully; for if the papyrus got damp it moulded and spoiled the writing, and if too dry it grew brittle and easily broke in handling. Then trouble came, as we shall find later, in St. Mark's Gospel, where it is likely the end piece cracked off and got lost and so caused trouble and manifold discussions in many ages since. In later times, when the position of the Epistles was recognized as Scripture, they were carefully copied on to parchment like the Old Testament. But they probably remained a good while on papyrus, and papyrus was a perilous material on which to preserve for the world the inspired Word of God.

§ 3. We have thirteen epistles of St. Paul. A third epistle to the Corinthians which he refers to [1] has evidently got lost, and possibly others. We have three epistles of St. John, one of James, one of Jude, a first epistle of Peter, and another called his Second Epistle, whose authorship is doubtful. The Epistle to the Hebrews is anonymous. It has been widely attributed to Paul, sometimes to Barnabas and others. Origen, the greatest Bible scholar the

[1] 1 Cor. v. 9.

world has seen, said of it in the third century, "Who wrote this epistle God only knows."

It is an interesting fact, and instructive too, as to the intercourse between churches and the gradual growth of the Canon of Scripture that St. Paul's were not the only Epistles to the Corinthians, Ephesians, Philippians, etc. Towards the close of St. John's life, Clement of Rome wrote his famous Epistle to the Corinthians, of which we get a glimpse again centuries later in a letter from the Corinthian Bishop Dionysius. "We have been reading in church to-day Clement's Epistle." About the same period Ignatius of Antioch on his way to martyrdom wrote epistles to the churches which he loved, and amongst them the Ephesians. Polycarp, the disciple of St. John, wrote an Epistle to the Philippians, and at its close (Ch. xiii.) he says, "I have received espistles from you and from Ignatius. You recommend me to send on yours to Syria; I shall do so either personally or otherwise. In return I send you the letter of Ignatius as well as others, which you ask for. . . . They will serve to edify your faith and perseverance."

These writers themselves, and doubtless the Church too, made a distinction between their letters and those of the Apostles. But it was not the sharp distinction of later days between Scripture and non-Scripture.

III

The Four Gospels.
Thus the Epistles were written. This brings us to about 65 A.D., thirty years after the Ascension. Not one of our Gospels was yet written. The larger churches had probably a collection of some Apostolic Epistles. These were the only documents.

But things could not go on thus much longer. Paul was dead. The men who had known Jesus were rapidly passing away. And all the time the Church was steadily growing in extent and needing to be told the Christian story. In the missionary churches amongst the heathen, where " they ordained elders in every city," there must be some authoritative documents for teachers to use who knew nothing at first hand of the Lord's life. Besides, it would hardly be safe to leave the story much longer, trusting to memory. For these were not quiet isolated people like the ancient Jews, with their traditions. The Church lived in the midst of bustling life and crowding events, a condition not favourable to long oral transmission.

So, just when Paul's Epistles and Paul's life were closing, begins the writing of our first three Gospels. Paul died about the year 64. The writing of our first Gospel is usually dated about 65.[1]

§ 2. The Oral Gospel had now become fairly fixed in men's memories. And scraps of writing were floating about. Some one here and there would write on a papyrus slip some saying of the Lord which especially touched him :—

JESUS SAID, COME UNTO ME, ALL YE WEARY, AND I WILL GIVE YOU REST.

JESUS SAID, A CERTAIN MAN HAD TWO SONS, ETC. (PRODIGAL SON).

JESUS SAID, BLESSED ARE THE PURE IN HEART, FOR THEY SHALL SEE GOD. BLESSED ARE THE PEACEMAKERS.

Amongst them was probably one which St. Paul had been taught, but which did not get into our Gospels.

JESUS SAID, IT IS MORE BLESSED TO GIVE THAN TO RECEIVE.[2]

And I like to think that in this form too came down that pathetic little story of Jesus and the Adulteress, which also was left out of the Gospels,

---

[1] Harnack (a famous present day investigator) has recently argued for an earlier date. He would put Mark between 50 and 60, Matthew about 70, and Luke in Paul's lifetime.

[2] Acts xx. 35.

but which appeals to every heart as a true story of Jesus. Some disciple who had heard it told in the oral teaching perhaps, wrote it down on a papyrus tablet. We hear that it was written into the lost "Gospel to the Hebrews." At any rate, some one who knew it, wrote it later on in a blank space in some copy of the Gospel manuscripts, and it so appealed to men's hearts that a place had to be made for it. The Revised Version indicates its unauthorized insertion into the middle of St. John's Gospel.[1] It evidently does not belong there, but wherever its true place the world has reason to be thankful to the man who wrote on his papyrus tablet long ago this lost story of Jesus.

Many of these little "Logia" or Sayings have recently been found in the East, some belonging to very early times, though not to the first century. Most of those found are already in the Bible. Some day we may light on a valuable collection in sealed jars or in tombs which will restore to us precious lost sayings of Jesus. The most interesting find up to this is that of the Oxyrinchus Papyri, found by Dr. Grenfell and Dr. Hunt at Oxyrinchus in Egypt in 1897 and 1903, now in the British Museum. They seem to preserve some lost sayings of Jesus which floated about in early evangelical tradition,

[1] St. John viii. 3.

but did not get into our Gospels. Quite an excitement was caused in 1903 at the discovery of the five sayings written on the back of a land surveyor's list of measurements and prefaced by the introduction, " These are the wonderful sayings of Jesus."

> JESUS SAITH, LET NOT HIM WHO SEEKS CEASE UNTIL HE FIND, AND WHEN HE FINDS HE SHALL BE ASTONISHED; ASTONISHED, HE SHALL REACH THE KINGDOM, AND HAVING REACHED THE KINGDOM HE SHALL REST.
>
> JESUS SAITH . . . AND THE KINGDOM OF HEAVEN IS WITHIN YOU, AND WHOSOEVER SHALL KNOW HIMSELF SHALL FIND IT (STRIVE THEREFORE) TO KNOW YRSELVES AND YE SHALL KNOW THAT YE ARE THE SONS OF THE FATHER, AND YE SHALL KNOW THAT YE ARE IN THE CITY OF GOD AND YE ARE THE CITY.[1]

§ 3. Probably there were little collections of these " sayings " which helped the writers of the Gospels. We know of one large collection attributed to St. Matthew, of which we shall hear more later.

---

[1] "Sayings of Our Lord," 2s., and "New Sayings of Jesus," 1s., published by Oxford University Press.

NEW "SAYINGS OF JESUS"
Papyrus from Oxyrhynchus, belonging to the Third Century A.D., now in the British Museum. By permission of the Egyptian Exploration Fund.

By and by would come something fuller—little Gospels, little attempts of private Christians to write down what they had been learning in church.

St. Luke's preface gives us a valuable glimpse of the position when he wrote. I quote from Revised Version :—

1. The Oral Gospel.	Even as they delivered them unto us which from the beginning were eye-witnesses and ministers of the Word.
2. The Fragmentary Gospels.	Forasmuch as many have taken in hand to draw up a narrative concerning those matters fully established among us.
3. The Final Gospels.	It seemed good to me also having traced the course of all things from the very first to write unto thee in order, most excellent Theophilus, that thou mightest know the certainty concerning the things wherein thou wast instructed by word of mouth.

Here we see the evolution of the first three Gospels : (1) the Oral Gospel ; (2) the Fragmentary Gospels ; (3) the Final Gospels as we have them. St. Luke sets himself to write *in order* the separate narratives which people were familiar with. Is it not very like the evolution in the Old Testament— the oral traditions followed by collections such as the Book of Jasher, and then by still fuller histories J and E and P, and all moving toward the complete Books as we have them to-day ?

§ 4. The first definite mention of our present Gospels is a very interesting one. Shortly after the death of St. John (about 120 A.D.) there was a bishop named Papias, Bishop of Hierapolis, in Phrygia. He lived close to apostolic days. He had met in Hierapolis the daughters of Philip the Evangelist, the virgins which did prophesy, who were friends of St. Paul.[1] Amongst his friends were Polycarp the disciple of St. John, and others who were acquaintances of the Twelve. (Irenæus says that Papias himself was a disciple of St. John.) He was very eager to learn everything they could tell him that the Apostles had said about Jesus. "For," he says, "I did not take pleasure as most people do in those who say a great deal, but in those that teach true things. I used to inquire what were the declarations of the elders, what Andrew or what Peter said, or what Philip or what Thomas or James, or what John or Matthew or what any other of the disciples of the Lord—and the things which Aristion and the elder (or presbyter) John the disciple of the Lord say. For I did not expect so much benefit from the contents of books as from the utterances of a living and abiding voice."

In view of what follows it is a very interesting

---

[1] Acts xxi. 9.

question, who is meant by the "elder" John. Papias speaks of the Apostles as "the elders," but why does he mention again an elder John? Is it another John, a presbyter or elder, or is it the Apostle already spoken of as an "elder"?[1] If the latter, as many scholars think, the following words should have great weight :—

John the Elder told Papias that Matthew wrote the "Logia," *i.e.* the Words or Sayings of Jesus, in Hebrew (*i.e.* Aramaic, the vernacular of Palestine). "And this too the Elder said, 'Mark, the interpreter of Peter, wrote down accurately, yet not in order, all that he (Peter) told as said or done by Christ. For he (Mark) himself did not hear the Lord nor was a disciple of His, but . . . of Peter, who used to give teachings to suit the immediate wants (of his hearers), but not as making a connected narrative . . . so that Mark made no mistake. . . . For he took care of one thing, not to leave out anything he heard nor give anything in a wrong way.'"[2]

§ 5. From this we gather that St. Matthew made a collection of discourses of Our Lord in Aramaic. No copy of this has yet been found. If

---

[1] Cf. Salmon, Introd., 90, 279.
[2] Eusebius, Eccl. Hist., III. 39.

ever it is, it will upset or confirm many theories made about it. It certainly was not our present Gospel of St. Matthew, though it probably formed the chief source for it.

The first Gospel was certainly St. Mark. Its basis apparently was the oral Gospel which he had learned in church on Sundays, especially the form in which he had heard Peter tell it. Where Mark wrote it, and why, and for what church, we do not know. But one thing we do know, that it meant more to the world than almost any other book written. For, as we shall see, it was also the chief source and foundation of the Gospels of St. Matthew and St. Luke. Just about twenty feet of papyrus roll easily injured in handling. The church which first got it had to be very careful not to break it, and in spite of all their care they apparently did break it—broke off a piece perhaps twelve inches long, which caused a good deal of trouble in later days. The Revised Version shows us how in the sixteenth chapter the Resurrection story breaks off awkwardly and abruptly at verse 8, and that an ending of twelve verses is added which quite probably does not belong there at all. The marginal note tells us that the oldest manuscripts omit this ending, and that different endings have been appended in several manuscripts. Evidently the reader who clumsily cracked off that piece is responsible for some confusion.

§ 6. Soon after St. Mark, appeared our First Gospel, called the Gospel of St. Matthew, probably because it was based largely on St. Matthew's collection of Discourses. Whether St. Matthew wrote it, or who wrote it in its present form, nobody really knows.

And very soon after came the Gospel of St. Luke, which he wrote with the Acts for some one called Theophilus. It does not seem very probable that two so great and valuable books so urgently needed by the whole Church should have been written for one private individual. The name Theophilus, Lover of God, or Beloved by God, may quite possibly be intended to mean any disciple. "The former treatise have I made, O Disciple, O Lover of God."

A careful study of these three Gospels brings out some curious facts as to their sources and composition. Matthew and Luke are the only Gospels that tell anything of the life of Jesus before His ministry began. There they write quite independently of each other, scarcely touching in any point.

The moment they begin the story of the Ministry they tell it in the same way, following mainly the order and frequently the very words of St. Mark.

Then when Mark comes to an end where the papyrus broke off at Ch. xvi. 8, they immediately branch out again, independently of each other and relating quite different incidents.

Volumes have been written on the difficult " synoptic problem," as it is called, of the composition of these synoptic Gospels. It is on the whole fairly evident that both used St. Mark, or an earlier version [1] of St. Mark, as a basis; that they had access to other sources, the chief probably being St. Matthew's collection of Sayings. But where did Luke get that immortal story of the " Shepherds abiding in the field," or those precious parables in Ch. xv., that " Gospel within the Gospel," or the many things in Ch. ix.–xviii. which seem to suggest a source known only to him? The early Church, as it attributed St. Mark's teaching to Peter, attributed St. Luke's teaching to Paul. Perhaps some of these things were in St. Paul's oral Gospel. Perhaps the earlier documents referred to in St. Luke's preface contained much to help him. The whole subject is still under discussion, though one

[1] Dr. Sanday would say a later version.

doubts if the discussions will lead us much further.

§ 7. Twenty-five years later comes the great Fourth Gospel, the Gospel of John. It differs materially from the other three. They were compilations made up of earlier existing material. This is an original work " dominated throughout by a great personality who has so meditated on the facts and truths he announces that they have been as it were recast in his own experience and bear traces everywhere of his genius."

St. John was at that time an old man living far away from the scenes of his boyhood. The young peasant of the Lake of Galilee is now the beloved bishop of the Church of Ephesus. But he is still in heart just " the disciple whom Jesus loved." The old man's eyes are ever turning back to that time, those three wonderful years when he had walked the fields of Galilee with his dear Lord, when, as he says, " we beheld His glory, the glory of the Only Begotten of the Father, full of grace and truth." James and Peter and Andrew and Philip are long since departed to be with their Master in the Unseen, and he is left alone brooding, as an old man will, on the precious memories of the past.

> "I'm growing very old. This weary head
> That hath so often leaned on Jesus' breast
> In days long by that seem almost a dream,
> Is bent and hoary with the weight of years.
> I'm old, so old, I cannot recollect
> The faces that I meet in daily life,
> But that dear Face and every word He spake
> Grow more distinct as others fade away,
> So that I live with Him and the holy dead
> More than the living."

§ 8. And how his people at Ephesus loved to hear the old man's memories of those years! They had probably at least one or more of the other three Gospels in writing. But it was so different to hear the living voice of their dear old bishop telling what he remembered. And he remembered so many things not written in their Gospels—his first meeting with Jesus; the marriage at Cana; the mysterious sacramental teaching about the Bread of God which cometh down from Heaven; the solemn Last Discourse at the First Communion; the story of the awful desolation when he saw Jesus dead; his personal memories of the Resurrection joy, especially of that exciting race for the tomb when he did outrun Peter; also his tender memories of the strange forty days which followed.

Year after year he had been telling them what he knew, and as he told it repeatedly the story grew into shape, and so there came the Gospel of St. John

—the Gospel of an old man's memories. He wrote it with the solemn purpose in his heart that " ye may believe that Jesus is the Christ, the Son of God ; and that believing ye may have life in His name." [1]

Probably it took years to write it. An old Church legend tells that in its final form a disciple of his, Prochorus, acted as his scribe, and several old manuscripts of his gospel have a picture of St. John raising his left hand towards the inspiring rays from Heaven and resting his right hand on the head of Prochorus, who is writing, " In the beginning was the Word."

Bishop Lightfoot suggests that the First Epistle of St. John's was written as a kind of covering letter in committing this Gospel to the Church, and at the close of the Gospel is an interesting authentication written perhaps by his own Church in Ephesus, " This is the disciple that testifieth of these things and wrote these things and we know that his testimony is true." [2]

So we close the touching story of that wonderful first century, taking us back to watch the beginnings of the Gospel, to live with those earnest simple-hearted men whose one central feeling was tender grateful personal love to Jesus. " Tell us about

[1] St. John xx. 31.   [2] St. John xxi. 24.

Jesus. Tell us what He said and did, how He looked and spake—our dear Lord who loved us and died for us."

May God the Holy Spirit touch our poor dull hearts and teach even to us also that personal love to Jesus!

CHAPTER II

THE CANON OF THE NEW TESTAMENT

I

How the Canon was formed. IN the making of the Old Testament we saw first the importance of the Divinely appointed, Divinely guided religious community, the Church, wherein, as in a cherishing home or nest, the Bible was to grow.

Then we saw that there were two stages of the making of the Bible in that community, which two stages must be carefully distinguished.

First, the gradual growth of a religious literature.

Second, the gradual selection or acceptance or recognition of certain parts of that literature by the Church as authoritative inspired Scripture.

This is true of the New Testament, equally with the Old, except that the process in the New Testament occupied but one generation, while in the Old it extended over nearly 2000 years.

§ 2. We have watched now the first stage, the growth of the Christian literature—the Epistles being written according as they were needed—the Gospels growing gradually like the Old Testament Books, oral tradition followed by fragmentary written summaries and completed by the writing of our present Four Gospels.

The Church then, about the year 100, had first and foremost its HOLY BIBLE, the authoritative inspired Books of the Old Testament. This was the sole "Canon of Scripture" in Apostolic days.

And it had also its RELIGIOUS LITERATURE, the Gospels, the Epistles, the Revelation of St. John, and also other religious books which ultimately found no place in Scripture. This literature was highly treasured and regarded as most valuable for edification, but certainly was not regarded as "Bible." Be it repeated again and carefully remembered, that to the first Christians, who were mainly Jews, the Holy Scriptures only meant the Old Testament Books. The name "Scripture" and the formula of quotation, "It is written," when used in the New Testament always refer to the Old Testament Books. They were the inspired Books, the prophecies of the coming of Christ, and with the imprimatur of Christ and the Apostles upon them as the authoritative Word of God. The

Christians of Apostolic days regarded these as their Bible, and had no intention of making any new Bible or adding anything to the old one.

The Christian literature was regarded as the human teaching of apostles and disciples, and was valued by them because of all it could tell about the ministry and life and death and Resurrection of that dear Lord whom they so deeply loved.

§ 3. Now we come to the second stage, the admission of the main part of this Christian literature into the Canon of Holy Scripture.

How did it come about? Practically in the same way as that of the Old Testament Books. Let me repeat what I said of them, that the Canon of Scripture was formed not suddenly by some startling miracle, not officially by some decision of Council or Synod or Bishop or Prophet or Saint, but slowly, gradually, half unconsciously by the quiet influence of the Holy Spirit on the minds of men in the Church. 'The Bible was formed even as the Church itself was formed, by that Holy Spirit which was the life of both.' But the mode of His working was by the quickening and guiding of human souls that they should instinctively love what was highest, that by a divine impulse they should gradually arrive at a general recognition of certain writings as authoritative and inspired Scripture.

As it was in the Old Testament, so was it also in the New. Humanly speaking, the matter was decided half unconsciously by usage - rather than by criticism or deliberate choice. Men in the Christian Church did not start out to make a new Bible or to add to the old one, but, almost before they knew, they had done it.

§ 4. It came about mainly through the READING OF THE LESSONS IN CHURCH. The question about any book was not whether it should be put into a Bible—that was not thought of at first—but whether it was worthy to be read in the Church services. We shall come later on a picture of these early Church services. They consisted of—

(1) Prayer, extempore or liturgical, with the Lord's Prayer as centre.

(2) Divine teaching, *i.e.* reading of the Old Testament.

(3) Human teaching—the preaching or exposition or the oral telling of the Gospel story.

(4) The celebration of Holy Communion.

Naturally at first the oral telling about Jesus which would be the sermon of the day—or the reading of one of the Epistles—would come under the head of Human Teaching. The little fragmentary written Gospel stories would naturally come under the same head, taking the place of the oral Gospel where no living witness of Jesus could be had. And quite probably the first three complete Gospels would take the same place at first, being only a sort of written sermon instead of an oral one. It is likely that St. John's Gospel sprang at once into the higher position of being read along with the Old Testament, since by that time the written Gospels seemed all moving up to that place.

§ 5. There is evidence for the belief that the Canon of the Gospels was the first part of the new Bible; that is to say, that they first rose into the position of being read along with the Divine Teaching (the Old Testament). As the years went on and the Lord had not returned, and the witnesses of His life and death and resurrection had passed away, these written Gospels became exceedingly precious to the Church. They were all they had of Jesus in permanent record. Whether written by Apostles or not, men felt that they contained at any rate *words of the Lord Jesus* which surely should rank higher than any word of Moses or the Prophets. Indeed, men must inevitably have felt that from the very first. And the sacredness attaching to the words of Jesus must have attached itself to the books which contained them. We should certainly be right in saying that this was the first step toward the accepting of the Gospels as Bible. So we are not surprised to find at the close of the first century the Gospels beginning to be read as Scripture in Church and quoted authoritatively in letters and sermons side by side with the words of the Old Testament Bible.

By the silent influence of the Holy Spirit in the Church the idea was quietly taking root of a new series of Divine authoritative documents. The formation of the New Testament had begun.

In the writings of the great Churchmen who came after the Apostles we can trace this most interesting process step by step. But I have no space to follow these separate steps. I can only glance here and there at points in the long line, three centuries long, which ended with the recognition of the complete New Testament.

II

Growth of Canon in First Century.
Our first glimpse is about the year 100 and just afterwards, about the time of St. John's death. Three great men stand out prominently in the Church. They had known and talked with the Apostles. They were successors of the Apostles in the rule of the Church. They lived far apart in the three provinces of the Church connected with the labours of St. Peter, St. Paul, and St. John. They were Clement of Rome, Ignatius of Antioch, and Polycarp of Smyrna, the disciple of St. John.

Irenæus, the great bishop of Lyons, later on tells us that "Clement had seen the blessed Apostles and conversed with them, and had the preaching of the blessed Apostles still sounding in his ears." Of Polycarp he says, "I can tell the place where the blessed Polycarp sat and taught and how he related his conversations with John and others who had seen the Lord, all of which he related agreeably to the Scriptures." I wish there were space to write more about him. Many readers will remember his touching words as they martyred him. "Revile Christ and you shall be free," cried the governor. "Ah, no," replied the dear old saint; "eighty and six years have I served Him, and He has never done me wrong. How can I blaspheme my King that saved me?" Ignatius, the third of these great fathers, is best known for the prominence which he gives to definite Church order and his evidence as to the established position of the Episcopate in the Church in his time, about A.D. 107.

But we are only concerned with their evidence as to the New Testament. There is a noble epistle of Clement to the Corinthians in which he quotes the Epistle of Paul to his own Roman Church, as also Paul's Epistle to the Corinthians, to whom he is writing. "Paul wrote you spiritually about himself and Cephas and Apollos because even then there were parties among you." He also, without quoting by name, makes use tacitly of many expressions which dictate his familiarity with other of our New Testament Books, especially St. John and Hebrews. Ignatius shows his knowledge of Corinthians, Galatians, and the Gospel of St. John. Polycarp in his one brief epistle has allusions to the Acts, 1 Peter, 1 John, Romans, Corinthians, Galatians, Ephesians, and 1 Timothy.

But (except Clement) they did not quote the books by name nor speak of them as Scripture. Their quotations from the Gospels are sometimes so indefinite that one suspects they may sometimes be only quoting from the Oral Gospel. Books did not seem to them so very important. Ignatius has one beautiful expression which bears on this point. " I have heard some say they would believe in the Gospel only as they found it in the records. To people of that kind I say, ' My authentic records are Jesus Christ, His Cross and Resurrection.' "

It is just as we might expect. The New Testament writings, though reverenced, are not yet thought of as Scripture. Yet these three great Churchmen, though they have not the slightest thought of putting them into the Bible, draw a line between them and their own writings as something on a far higher level. " I cannot write with authority," says Clement, " like the blessed Paul, who wrote spiritually." " One like me," says Polycarp, " cannot attain to the wisdom of the blessed Paul." " Peter and Paul were Apostles," says the dying Ignatius. " I am but a poor condemned man." Thus silently and slowly in far separate parts of the Church was beginning the recognition of the greatness of the Scriptures.

§ 2. Move on fifty years. Justin Martyr is a prominent name in the Roman Church. He was born about the year 100, about the time that St. John died. It was probably about the year 140 that he wrote his famous " Apology " to the Emperor, which gives a valuable picture of early Church life. " On the day of the Sun (Sunday) all those of us who live in the same town or district assemble together, and there is read to us some part of the Memoirs of the Apostles, which " (he says elsewhere) " are called Gospels, and the Writings of the Prophets as much as time permits. Thus whoever is presiding gives us a sermon, after which we rise for common prayer; afterwards bread and wine are brought," etc.

What concerns us here is the explicit statement that about forty years after St. John's death the Gospels are being regularly read along with the Old Testament. Nay, they are even mentioned before them as if even more important. This is a clear indication of the growing recognition of their position as Scripture.

§ 3. Twenty years later, A.D. 160, we have an important proof of the high position in the Church of our Four Gospels. It is a curious Church book by Tatian, a disciple of Justin Martyr. It is called the " Diatessaron, or Book of the Four." In it he weaves together into one continuous story the narratives of the four Gospels, omitting all repetitions, so as to make a connected Life of Christ. This was a very convenient book to have when the Gospels were four separate rolls, and one had to pass from one to the other to get the whole story. I have given an extract from it on page 110.

It was widely used for Church reading, especially in the Syrian Church to which Tatian belonged. In fact, for centuries it superseded there the separate four Gospels. We learn that it was read along with the Old Testament. A bishop some centuries later says that he found two hundred copies of it in the churches of his diocese, and ordered them to be changed for copies of the separate Gospels. It shows at any rate that the Four Gospels were now standing out clearly on a level by themselves as the chief Lesson Books of the Church.

Still, there seems no thought of making a new Bible; only carefulness about books to be read in church. But as we go on, we find more and more the Gospels being read beside the Law, and the Epistles beside the Prophets, the continuing of the long process which went on until the whole New Testament was complete as "Bible."

§ 4. Now comes a very important document for our purpose, an old, torn, mutilated fragment, date about 170 A.D., discovered several years ago in the Ambrosian Library of Milan. It is called the Muratorian Fragment, and contains at any rate the earliest list in existence of the Church books, if it be too much to call it the first known judgment of the Catholic Church as to the books of her New Testament.

It almost certainly must have begun by mentioning St. Matthew and St. Mark as the first and second Gospels, for this torn piece begins by telling us that " the Gospel of St. Luke, the physician, companion of St. Paul, stands third." The fourth place it assigns to the Gospel of St. John, " a disciple of the Lord who wrote at the request of his fellow-disciples and bishops. As he says in his epistle, ' What we have seen with our eyes and heard with our ears and our hands have handled of the Word of Life.' For so he professes that he was not only an eyewitness, but also a hearer."

After the Gospels it places the Acts. Then the thirteen Epistles of Paul, pointing out that " though four of them, Philemon, Titus, 1 and 2 Timothy, were written from personal feeling and affection, yet they are hallowed in the respect of the Catholic Church."

" Moreover," it adds, " there is in circulation an Epistle to the Laodiceans and one to the

Alexandrians forged in Paul's name and several others which cannot be received in the Catholic Church. The Epistle of Jude, however, and two with the name of John are held in the Catholic Church. We receive also the Revelation of John and the Revelation of Peter, which latter some of our body will not allow to be read in Church."

This old fragment is very valuable not only for the distinction it notes between our books of Scripture and the other books, but especially as showing that about seventy years after the Apostles nearly all our present New Testament was in use as Scripture. It omits the Epistles of James, 1 and 2 Peter, and Hebrews, which were not universally known and accepted for some time after this. And it tells of other books which still hung on the borderland, such as the Revelation of Peter, etc.

III

The Close of the Second Century. Three great Churchmen stood at the beginning of this century, Clement, Ignatius, and Polycarp. Three other great Churchmen fittingly close it, who, like the first three, lived far apart, and thus are the more valuable as witnesses to the growth of the New Testament. They are—

Irenæus of Lyons in the south of France.
Clement of Alexandria in distant Egypt.
Tertullian of the rude church of Northern Africa.

§ 1. Irenæus was a native of Asia Minor, was in close contact with Rome, and was (about 180 A.D.) Bishop of Lyons in Gaul; therefore his evidence is of more value than that of men whose horizon was more limited. He tells us of his youthful recollections of Smyrna and of its great old bishop Polycarp, the disciple of St. John. He remembers where the old man used to sit and teach, and how he spoke of St. John and others who had seen the Lord, how he used to repeat from memory what they told him about the Lord, and, adds Irenæus, "all that he said was in strict agreement with *the Scriptures.*" Evidently, then, the Gospels had now been firmly established in their position as "Scriptures," and the connection of Irenæus with St. John through Polycarp reminds us that this had taken place while still in touch with that age when men lived who had known Jesus.

But he has stronger expressions than this. He

quotes St. Matthew i. 18, and says, "The Holy Spirit said by Matthew, 'The birth of Christ was on this wise,'" thus asserting his and evidently the Church's belief in the inspiration of the Gospels. And perhaps stronger still is his curious mystical explanation why the Gospels are four and only four. As there are four chief winds and four regions of the world, and four pillars of the earth, and four faces to the cherubim on which rested the Divine presence, so Christ gave His Gospels in a fourfold form, and on these four Gospels He rests. We may smile at his fanciful argument, but his evidence is quite clear that in his day at any rate our four Gospels and no others were recognized by the Church at large, and that they were regarded as the inspired Scriptures of God.

Of the other books of the New Testament he quotes repeatedly as Scripture the Acts, twelve Epistles of Paul (omitting Philemon), the Revelation of St. John, and also 1 John and 1 Peter and Hebrews. The other books he says nothing about, but it is worth notice as showing that the boundary-line of the New Testament was not yet drawn, that he also quotes as Scripture an apocryphal book, the Shepherd of Hermas.

§ 2. Now from the old French city we move far away to the East, to that great seat of learning, the city of Alexandria, which we have already seen in our story of the Apocrypha. Clement, the bishop, is a scholar, and has travelled widely and visited many churches. His master and predecessor, Pantaenus, was a very old man, and probably had known men who were friends of the Apostles. So Clement, like Irenæus, is in touch with apostolic times, and he affirms in his great book, the "Patchwork" (*Stromata*), that his writings contain "the shadow and outline of what he had heard from men who preserved the true tradition of the blessed doctrine directly from Peter and James, from John and Paul, the holy Apostles."

Here we have the oral Gospel and the written books side by side, and it must always be remembered as a guarantee of accuracy that the written Gospels came into use during the lifetime of that generation who had known the Apostles and some of whom had known the Lord Himself.

Clement has a sentence which is valuable for our purpose. Speaking of one of the lost "Sayings of Jesus," he says, "We have not this saying in the four Gospels which have been handed down to us; it is found in the gospel according to the Egyptians." Here are our four Gospels again standing out prominently by themselves. Beside the four Gospels he quotes the Acts, twelve epistles of St. Paul, omitting Philemon), the Epistle to the Hebrews (which he says is by St. Paul), 1 John, 1 Peter, Jude, and the Revelation of St. John. But again it must be noted that he also quotes, as inspired, books not now received the epistles of Clement and Barnabas, the Revelation of Peter and the Shepherd, thus indicating that the Church has not yet drawn a line of demarcation around its Scriptures.

§ 3. From Alexandria we move westward to the old historic Carthage. In the Church of that place is a presbyter famous in history. Trained as a lawyer in the secular courts, learned, able, eager after God and righteousness, but one of those restless, impetuous spirits who are the despair of those set over them, and the wholesome terror of those who oppose them. Such men are often valuable champions in any cause. Such was this man Tertullian.

We are not concerned here with his life and character, which I only refer to because I want him to be something more to the reader than a mere name. For us he is here merely a witness. We want to know what he and his Church thought with regard to the growing New Testament. He tells us that the Epistles of St. Paul have been preserved in the churches which he founded; so, too, the four Gospels have been handed down to us in due succession on the authority of the Apostolic Churches. The next thing we find is that there is already a Latin Version of the books in his church, for he grumbles at it, as he does at many other things. It is a clumsy translation. But that does not matter to us. See what it means, that at the end of the second century not only are the principal books of the New Testament accepted throughout the Church, but translations of them are already known and recognized.

Tertullian's quotations cover pretty much the whole ground of his Latin Testament, which contains all our present books except the Epistles of James, 2 Peter, and Hebrews.

At this stage, then, about 200 A.D., the position of the New Testament is practically established; all its principal books are everywhere received and used as Scripture. Therefore with regard to them the discussion may now close. All that remains to be studied is the gradual drawing of the boundary-line. There are seven minor books, James, 2 Peter, 2 and 3 John, Jude, Hebrews, and Revelation, which are accepted and used in some churches, but not universally; and there are a few apocryphal books, such as Clement, Barnabas, Hermas, afterwards omitted from the Canon of Scripture, but which still hang on the border. With regard to the seven disputed books, we must not exaggerate the position. The fact that they were not everywhere received is sometimes only because they were small and addressed to private persons, and therefore did not come much under the notice of the Church; or sometimes because a book well known and honoured in one place was very little known in another. For example, the Epistle to the Hebrews on this list was known and highly honoured in Rome from the days of Clement, before St. John died. But, on the other hand, 2 Peter was suspected as of doubtful authenticity even where it was well known.

Be it remembered, then, that we have no further concern except with these few questioned books on the border-line.

IV

The Great Persecution, A.D. 303.

We pass over 100 years. We are in the midst of the terrible persecution of the Church by the Emperor Diocletian. Life had been too easy for Christians, and they became proud and careless. Like a bolt out of the blue came the Imperial edict that the churches should be razed to the ground and the Scriptures consumed by fire. All over the Church was excitement and trouble and fear and fierce, passionate determination that their sacred Scriptures should not be yielded to the infidel. It was a bitter struggle, and they suffered sorely. "I saw," says Eusebius, the great Church historian (note his name, for he will come prominently before us again), "I saw with my own eyes the houses of prayer thrown down and razed to their foundations and the inspired and sacred Scriptures consigned to the fire in the open market-place." Many brave men laid down their lives rather than yield their Holy Writings. Many others bought safety by a pretended submission, giving up as Scriptures books which were not accepted by the Church. These were hated and scorned as "traditores," traitors, and so arose anger and bitterness and separations. It was a very miserable time.

It brings back for us the similar awful times in the Old Testament days, when Antiochus was destroying the Scriptures of the Law. And in a similar way, in the loving providence of God, good came also out of this terrible evil. When life was the price of preserving the Scriptures and when men were excusing themselves by the plea that the books surrendered were not really Scripture, it naturally tended towards definiteness in deciding the limits of the accepted books. What books were " Canonical Scriptures " ? What books were not ? From this time forward the word Canonical became a familiar word and the wavering border-line tended to become fixed.

Yet, strange to say, even at such a crisis there was no definite concerted action of the Church, no definite synodical statement determining the exact boundaries of the New Testament. For which we may be thankful. For no single decision of any body of men would have the weight that comes from the silent conviction of many generations on whose consciences the Sacred Writings were winning their way.

V

The First Christian Bibles.

A quarter of a century has elapsed. We are with the Church in Palestine. The time is A.D. 331. The place is the Scriptorium, where manuscripts were written in the library of Eusebius, the Bishop of Cæsarea, the same Eusebius, the great Church historian who has so lately been watching the Scriptures burned in the fire (p. 204).

There is eager activity amongst the scribes. Every desk is occupied. They are proud men to-day, for a high honour has been conferred on the Scriptorium of Cæsarea. A letter has come from the Emperor Constantine to the bishop. He wants to make a royal present to the churches of Constantinople, and he requests the bishop "that you bid fifty copies of the Divine Scriptures to be written on prepared skin, by skilled scribes who are well acquainted with their craft. For this purpose orders have been issued to the governor of the province to furnish everything required, and two public carriages are to be employed for conveying the books to the Emperor."

It was a nice book order to get, especially where expense did not matter and the men who loved to make beautiful books could spend time and money freely. There was good reason why the order should come to Cæsarea. For the most celebrated Christian library in the world was there, the library of Pamphilus, who was the predecessor of Eusebius. We have some manuscripts of later days, in which as a badge of high honour the inscription is in the margin, "This has been compared with the copy in Cæsarea in the library of the holy Pamphilus."

More important still is the fact that the bishop himself, Eusebius, is a great biblical scholar, and has made wide research on the whole subject of the accepted and non-accepted books. Perhaps that day when he watched the burning Scriptures impressed him with the need of investigating the subject thoroughly.

§ 2. It is not easy to find out from his account what he exactly believed on the subject. Like many another author who had too great a plethora of facts to digest, he probably could not quite make up his mind. Or, rather, since he is aiming not to tell his own opinion, but the opinion of the universal Church and that universal Church had made no definite pronouncement, he had to be rather vague and sometimes contradictory.

He divided the writings which claimed a place in Scripture into three classes—

(1) The *Accepted Books*, which practically includes the whole New Testament, the exceptions being some of the seven books which I have referred to (p. 203).

(2) *The Controverted Books, i.e.* books received in some places and not in others; the Epistles of James and Jude, 2 and 3 John, and 2 Peter. He is puzzled and undecided about the Book of Revelation, but on the whole thinks it should be considered as accepted.

(3) *The Spurious Books*, in which he includes the Epistle of Barnabas and the Shepherd of Hermas, though he thinks rather favourably of them.

§ 3. Now must have come to him the serious question, What books are to go into the Emperor's Bible? For such a group of such splendid Bibles and under the patronage of the Emperor would be likely to have a considerable effect on the usage of the Churches.

But he says nothing about this, nor does he tell us exactly how he fulfilled the Emperor's order. We should greatly like to get hold of one of his books and to be absolutely certain that it was one of them.

THE SINAITIC MANUSCRIPT

Probably one of the Bibles made for the Emperor by Eusebius.

Naturally in the discoveries of ancient manuscripts men have been looking for these Bibles. It has been conjectured,[1] and it would seem with some reason, that we have at least one of them, and perhaps two.

Eusebius says that he had the Bibles written triple and quadruple—by threes and fours, a puzzling expression which has been conjectured to mean three and four columns on a page. Now the two oldest Bibles in the world are the Vatican manuscript in the Vatican Library at Rome and the Sinaitic so romantically discovered by Dr. Tischendorf about fifty years ago in the convent of St. Catherine on Mount Sinai, and these are written respectively three and four columns on a page. Dr. Tischendorf believed that a certain handwriting in one of these appears also in the other, which, if so, would look as if they came from the same Scriptorium. The Sinaitic shows the marks of several correctors, and one of these, supposed to be about the seventh century, has written after the books of Ezra and Esther :—" This has been compared with a very old copy collated by the hand of the holy martyr Pamphilus, which at the end has the subscription . . . I, Pamphilus

---

[1] Cf. Gregory, "Canon and Text," p. 327. Souter, "Text and Canon," p. 22.

corrected."[1] Evidently, therefore, this manuscript must in the seventh century have been at Cæsarea, where Eusebius' Bibles were made.

Now if this be really one of Eusebius' Bibles, it is a valuable find in this investigation. For it contains exactly our present New Testament Books, and at the end of them the two apocryphal books, Barnabas and Hermas, which from their position look as if they were regarded as an appendix. The Vatican Manuscript, having lost all the pages after Heb. ix. 14, is no use at all for our purpose, even if it be one of the Emperor's Bibles.

VI

Athanasius and Jerome.
Thirty years later. It is Easter Day, A.D. 365, in the city of Alexandria. In all the churches of the city the clergy are reading to their people the Easter Pastoral Letter of their great archbishop Athanasius, the champion who saved the Church from heresy. Every year he has issued his Pastoral, but this year it is especially noteworthy for its clear, definite pronouncement about the Canonical Scriptures.

[1] Souter, p. 23.

"I shall use for the support of my boldness," says the Archbishop, "the model of the evangelist Luke and say as he does, Forasmuch as some have taken in hand to set forth in order for themselves the so-called Apocrypha and to mix these with the inspired Scriptures, which we most surely believe, even as they delivered it to our fathers, which from the beginning were eye-witnesses and ministers of the Word; it seemed good to me also having been urged by true brethren . . . to publish the books which are admitted in the canon, and have been delivered unto us, and are believed to be divine," etc.

Then, after giving a full list of the Old Testament Books, relegating the Apocrypha to a sort of appendix, he turns to give a list of the New Testament, and *this list is exactly that of our New Testament to-day.*

§ 2. We now move from the churches of Palestine and Egypt to the church in the centre of the civilized world at Rome—and from the great scholars and churchmen Eusebius and Athanasius to the still greater scholar and churchman, Jerome. In 383, at the request of Pope Damasus, he began the revision of the "old Latin" New Testament, the beginning of the work which is his monument for ever, the great Vulgate Bible. It was called Vulgate or common when it became the common Bible of the Western Church. For 1000 years it was practically the Bible of all Europe; therefore when we say that *the Books of its New Testament are exactly what we have to-day*, we may consider our inquiry closed as to the growth of the Canon. The question as to what Books should constitute the New Testament will never be opened again.

So we close our story of the Making of the Bible. In one sense it has shown us that the Church made the Bible. The Church by her great sons received the inspired words; the Church through many ages decided its contents. But I trust it has shown more clearly the awe-inspiring truth that the Bible was made for man by the Holy Spirit of God. He it was who gave the holy words to His Church. He it was who by His silent influence on that Church decided what its contents should be. Surely it was no chance that made the Canon of Scripture. For if anything is clearly taught by this story it is this, which I said at its beginning, that the Canon of Scripture was formed not suddenly by some startling miracle, not officially by some decision of Synod or Bishop or prophet or saint, but slowly, gradually, half unconsciously, by the quiet influence of the Holy Spirit on the minds of men in the Church. The Bible was formed even as the Church itself was formed, by that Holy Spirit who was the life of both.[1]

[1] Bishop Westcott.

God made the Bible. God made the Old Testament. God made the New. And when "in the fulness of time God sent forth His Son" His hand united them. At His feet they touched each other. The Old Bible is the preparation for Him. The New is the interpretation of Him. Let no man neglect the Old because of present-day difficulties. Let no man neglect the Old because the New is higher. They belong to each other and are dependent on each other. The whole Bible is as one great temple 2000 years in building. "The Old Testament is the nave with its side aisles of psalm and prophecy; and the Gospels as the choir, the last Gospel perhaps the very sanctuary, while around and behind are the Epistles and the Apocalypse each a gem of beauty, each supplying an indispensable feature in the majestic whole."[1] God give us grace to use it!

Blessed Lord, who hast caused all holy Scriptures to be written for our learning: Grant that we may in such wise hear them, read, mark, learn and inwardly digest them, that by patience, and comfort of Thy holy Word, we may embrace and ever hold fast the blessed hope of everlasting life which Thou hast given us in our Saviour Jesus Christ. Amen.

[1] Canon Liddon.

The Latest Book on Palestine

Palestine and the World

By F. G. Jannaway, Author of "Palestine and the Jews," "Palestine and the Powers," "British Museum with Bible in Hand," etc., etc. Crown 8vo. Wrapper. Profusely illustrated with photographs and plan. 7/6 net.

Mr. Jannaway has just returned from his fifth visit to the Land and has brought back the latest information upon this burning question and ambition of the Zionists.

The British Museum with Bible in Hand

By F. G. Jannaway.

Crown 8vo. Cloth. Profusely Illustrated. 2/- net.

A facsimile of a complimentary letter from Sir Frederick C. Kenyon, K.C.B., LL.D., etc., Director and Principal Librarian of the British Museum, appears in the work.

Palestine Pictured

or, WHERE HE DWELT

By Alfred T. Schofield

Containing 43 illustrations from photographs taken specially for this work, and a coloured map. Crown 8vo. Cloth. 2/6 net.

Delightful as a book of travel and also valuable as a companion volume for students of the New Testament. The language is simple and graphic.

SAMPSON LOW, MARSTON & COMPANY, LTD.
100, Southwark Street. London.

NEW EDITION

The Emphasised New Testament

BY

JOSEPH BRYANT ROTHERHAM

Cloth. Seven Shillings and Sixpence net
Full Morocco. Fifteen Shillings net

THE PLACE FILLED BY "THE EMPHASISED NEW TESTAMENT."

During the last half-century, the mind of the Bible-reading public has, to an encouraging extent, been weaned from a merely superstitious regard for the accustomed form of words in Bible translation, and become impressed with the importance of getting as near as possible to the meaning of the originals.

For the attainment of this end, a comparison of various translations has been found very helpful; bondage to the letter being thereby replaced by a clearer insight into the spirit and meaning of our Sacred Writings.

Several translations of the New Testament prepared the way for the appearance of the Revision of 1881. All these were mainly literal in character. They have been followed by some Free Versions in Modern English; which, in their turn, have done excellent service, partly by showing how chastely and even elegantly, in present day style, Divine truths can be expressed, and partly by meeting the needs of Sunday School Teachers by assisting them to clothe in simple language those sweet stories of old which children so well love to hear. The one great weakness of these free versions is, that they tend to expand and colour the meaning, rather as inferred by the translator than as actually present in the original.

Under these circumstances "The Emphasised New Testament" maintains its unique and useful place. It is extremely literal, and for that very reason yields the keenest pleasure to sympathetic minds, just because it gives the drift, point and emphasis of the original—the very feeling of the Greek being clearly discernible in English. It is confidently believed that, in this respect, it has no equal in our language.

Besides its value as a translation, it—now, in its later editions—possesses the additional merit of being so set forth on the page as to reveal at once, not only the transitions from narrative to speech and the like, but also the interruptions and digressions so characteristic of the Pauline Epistles, the eye being thus guided to trace the main course of the argument.

The translator was spared to revise his work, thus securing for the latest edition the highest attainable accuracy and usefulness.

LONDON: SAMPSON LOW, MARSTON AND COMPANY, LTD.

www.ingramcontent.com/pod-product-compliance
Lightning Source LLC
Chambersburg PA
CBHW021824230426
43669CB00008B/858